THE PROMISE

THE PROMISE

POSITIONED & PREPARED TO RECEIVE

KEITH GARNER

THE PROMISE Copyright © 2015 by Keith Garner.

This book is a work of fiction. Names, characters, businesses, organizations, places, events and incidents either are the product of the author's imagination or are used fictitiously. Any resemblance to actual persons, living or dead, events, or locales is entirely coincidental.

For information contact;

Keith Garner

www.keithgarner.com

Book and Cover design by Victoria Fleary

ISBN: 978-0-9964202-0-4

First Edition: May 2015

10 9 8 7 6 5 4 3 2 1

This book is dedicated to the family and friends who has continuously believed and encouraged me to push until the ideas conceived in my heart are manifested in my life. Your faith and love demonstrated throughout the years helped fuel my passion to deliver to the world a glimpse of the gifts God, my Creator has deposited in my spirit.

CONTENTS

PREPARED FOR MY PROMISE   1

PREPARATION EMULATES GOD   21

PREPARATION DEVELOPS
AND REQUIRES DISCIPLINE   24

PREPARATION ESTABLISHES STRUCTURE   37

PREPARATION GENERATES MOMENTUM   43

PREPARATION PRODUCES PATIENCE   51

PREPARATION HELPS POSITION YOU   55

PROVOKE THE HEAVENS TO RESPOND   67

ABOUT THE AUTHOR   86

—————○ ● ○—————

God waits for our faith to move us toward Him so He can begin to move our promise towards us.

—————○ ● ○—————

PREPARED FOR MY PROMISE

I BELIEVE EVERY INDIVIDUAL EVER CREATED SINCE the beginning of time will receive at least one promise in his or her lifetime. I am not talking about a person's destiny, but a simple promise. Whether it is a promise of marriage, children, career, inheritance, business opportunity, car, money, travel, or any other imaginable desire you can conjure. In the King James Version of the Bible, the word promise is found 13 times. However, theologians say there are more than 3,500 promises delineated in the Holy Scriptures for mankind. If there are so many promises outlined in the Scriptures, why does it seem as if it is the ones that do not come innately that causes so much concern?

I am truly appreciative and grateful for the God-inspired scriptures provided for us to read, study and understand the promises God laid up for us. For if our promise was never communicated, we would not have the opportunity to be made aware, and how could we ever expect it? If we never expect you promise, why should you prepare for it? If you never prepare for it, how will you be able to keep and prosper in it once you receive it? Most of all, the Scriptures provide record of a promise-making God, and a promise-keeping God. This helps us to become more familiar with the One making the promise, rather focusing on the kinds of promises that were not only made but also kept.

How does one prepare for something they have never seen before? How will you be able to recognize your promise when it arrives or manifests? Better yet, how does one prepare for something they cannot truly fathom? To obtain a more in-depth understanding of this concept, let's see what constitutes preparation. How is preparation birth in the spirit of man?

There is much insight and revelation to be found in the first two chapters of Genesis as it pertains to preparation. As you dissect these passages, you should begin to realize that God really does know your end before your beginning. With this in mind, it offers a methodology or pattern for how God establishes things in the earth. It tells us that before you can legitimately begin the process of preparation, you first must possess the ability to see the end state of your life with your promise. This is ability or gift is simply known as vision. Vision is defined as *the ability to think about or plan the future with imagination or wisdom*. This is the very essence of the creation of earth and man. God demonstrating his ability to imagine something, then speak it into existence. Simply put, God saw the end from the beginning [Is 46:10], thus enabling Him to order His creation in a manner where everything was prepared for His most precious creation of all; man.

I believe every man, woman and child have been given the gift of vision, and it merely has to be cultivated. In today's culture, many of our children's dreams have been crushed and stifled at a young age. Our children, the next generation largely has not been taught how to dream, or how to envision themselves beyond their current economic condition or surroundings. Far too often have they been told their aspirations and goals are far-fetched, unattainable, thus smothering the affluent seeds by creating a nutrient deficient environment for them to grow. The dry and desolate atmospheres these children are living inhibit many of their abilities to develop a vision of their desired future. If these conditions remain, it could rob the earth of a bright and prosperous future.

Preparation is essential to achieving any predestined or predetermined goal. *Webster's Dictionary defines the word prepare as to make (something) ready for us or consideration; created in advance; preplanned.* This definition merely gives us a foundation for what we must do to seize our promise. In order to learn how to prepare, we must first obtain a deeper understanding of the word prepare. The word "pre" is defined as a prefix or preposition in its usage, meaning before or previous. This word literally signifies time, place, order or importance. King Solomon was known as the wisest man in the Bible, and he provided us with great insight concerning life and God in the book of Ecclesiastes. He tells us "There is an opportune time to do things, a right time to do things on the earth" [Msg]. Therefore, the art of preparation not only requires time and dedication, but also the understanding of times and seasons.

The second half of the word is "pare", which denotes the act of cutting or trimming away the outer edges of a thing, or reduce in size. If you have ever spent any time in the kitchen, you are familiar with a paring knife. A paring knife is a small, sharp knife designed for peeling fruits and vegetables. If you were to place this tool in the hand of a chef, he or she could transform the very shape and appearance of the fruit or vegetable with this one little knife. When we submit our lives to the Lord, and allow for Him to prepare us for that the promise He has designed for us, He will transform your entire being. God does this with His word. Hebrews 4:12 "God means what he says. What he says goes. His powerful Word is sharp as a surgeon's scalpel, cutting through everything, whether doubt or defense, laying us open to listen and obey."

It is a necessity to make your life ready to achieve and receive every goal and promise pertaining to your life and legacy. My former pastor, the late Robert L. Macklin, often said, "preparation precedes the blessing." Of course, like many of us when we're young, I really did not understand this old adage, nor did I seek any understanding from the one who said it. While it sounded nice, and possessing a memorable rhythm, it did not strike a cord with me until I was much older. It was not until I had a desire that was beyond my reach, beyond my human ability. This desire wasn't some mere fleshly desire burning within me; it was ignited by a promise found in the word of God. It was as if I was reaching for the moon with dinosaur arms. The more I reached for this promise; the more wind filled my hands.

To properly prepare for your destiny or promise, you must possess an accurate vision of your expected end embracing your promise. How can one successfully prepare for something they have not seen? When an artist begins his or her work on a painting, they have an image of the final picture; even a musician has a particular sound of the song they are attempting to manufacture. It is vital to possess the assurance and wherewithal to not just plan a future with the inhabitation of one's promise, but to have a vision of the end state as a reference to strive towards. This concept benefits you by identifying the time required to gather the pertinent resources for the expectant season ahead, and then you can begin to put them in place.

Preparation is not only fundamental to the life of a true believer, but to any human being upon the face of the earth. When I use the term true believer, I am not merely referring to a believer in God, but someone who has chosen to believe in something greater than them. Preparation is a part of every individual's life, whether we acknowledge it or not. Regardless of your age, either someone has helped you to prepare for something, or you have taken it upon yourself to prepare on your own. You have prepared for bedtime. You prepare for dinner. Majority of the world dedicates weeks preparing for Christmas and Thanksgiving Day. If you ask an entertainer, whether musician or sports, what does it take to become great, they would most likely tell you it requires much preparation.

One must understand the art of preparation in order to achieve that which you believe is destined to come into your life. There must be purposeful actions married to your faith that are strategically assigned to the various elements of the vision of your promise produced by your hope. This kind of faith in action should birth a wealth of excitement in the life of a believer. The joy is not merely a result of the vision of the promise hoped for, but the enjoyment of undergoing the preparation process. It is this process that begins to exposes the evidence of your promise becoming a true reality.

"By failing to prepare, you are preparing to fail." This is a famous quote of one of the most influential and important men, not only in the United States of America, but also had a profound impact on the world at large. Benjamin Franklin was a writer, philosopher, inventor, politician, scientist, publisher and a Founding Father of the United States of America. As a scientist, he helped the world to move forward with his discoveries about electricity, and lent his wisdom for almost two decades to the colonies as they set out to build a bright new world of freedom and idealism. With this phrase, Benjamin Franklin was telling us that when you know and understand what you have you sights set on, you should not only plan for it, but also prepare. When you make the conscious or unconscious decision not to prepare, you have consequently prepared yourself to fail.

In as much, weddings and funerals take a lot of preparation and often times money. The preparation for a child also requires much time and attention, especially if it is your first. There tends to be much anxiety and concerns with this being unchartered territory for the mother and father. The woman's body experiences a variety of changes to its form and appetite. If executed properly, the preparation for a family vacation could require a significant amount of time and energy. Dependent upon where, when and how the travel will be performed, certain details must be accounted for. The important things in life, we commonly see that there is some level of preparation involved. Conversely, I am fully persuaded that even the smallest things in life require preparation. While the small things in life usually have little consequences when failing to prepare at the time of encounter, they rarely seem important until you are confronted with a situation and no apparent solution within grasp. However, I will remind you of one of the most profound statements from the wisest man to have lived:

Song of Solomon 2:15 "Take us the foxes, the little foxes, that spoil the vines; for our vines have tender grapes."

This passage reminds me to be mindful of the smallest of things, because if ignored, they could have major consequences. The little foxes, the babies, were so small they could not reach the grapes on the vines would nibble on the entire vine until they fell to the ground, thus ruining the harvest. It is one thing if they just picked the grapes from the vine, but when you destroy the vine itself, the entire reproductive system is damaged. Most farmers would typically uproot the vine and start replanting seeds due to the uncertainty of the vine's ability to regenerate. Due to the farmer's negligence of not accounting for the little foxes, they have not only lost a harvest, but also lost time and the possibility of multiple seasons of reproduction from one vineyard.

Every person's life can benefit from the slightest bit of preparation.

For instance, always keeping a little cash just in case your credit card is not approved or the computer is malfunctioning while attempting to make a purchase. Maybe outfitting your home with a fire extinguisher in the event a fire breaks out in your home. Even stocking up on non-perishable foods, water, toiletries and other items necessary in the event of a disaster would be another reason to prepare. Honestly, there are multiple motives an individual would see the need to prepare which would increase their chances for success in whatever the given endeavor.

With life being filled with some many ups and downs, preparation is crucial to maximizing your successes and minimizing your failures. By applying sound preparation does not exclude you from suffering some failures, but it does limit them and provide additional data points to avoid repeating the same shortcomings. Whether big or small, significant or trivial, you must decide how much you are willing to risk if you do not take the time to prepare for your destiny. Understanding we have a finite lifespan, we cannot be completely prepared for every little occurrence in our lives, but we must begin to put some things in place to direct our lives.

Lack of preparedness has a cost. By not preparing, you could either forfeit a prosperous future, or not be able to sustain it. Either way, you will walk away from the experience feeling as if the world has collapsed all around you. Often times, the challenge is not always being able to seize the very thing you are striving for, but possessing the ability to keep it. The act and mentality of preparation creates a structure to house promise you are longing for. It establishes a foundation on which you will stand as it hoists you up to grab hold of the thing that has been beyond your fingertips.

What are the places in your life where failure is not an option? Is there an area in life where people are dependent upon your success?

While you may have done some things to prepare, but was it the proper amount to avoid failure. Some things may not be prevented, but other times failure happens because the smallest thing may be missing as a result of unpreparedness.

How important must something be in order for you to take the time to create a plan? How much greater is its importance to your life before you commence preparations for it come into your life? How often do you evaluate your preparations and progress as things in your life changes? What cost are you willing to pay for your lack of preparedness? What cost, in addition to pain and anguish, are you willing to allow your family and friends to incur for your unwillingness to prepare?

———————— ○ ● ○ ————————

The amount of faith an individual possesses and is willing to put on display will ultimately decide the release of your promise.

———————— ○ ● ○ ————————

I believe that in order for you to become excited about making the necessary preparations in your life to obtain your promise, you first must have a clear understanding of the promise you are seeking after. Webster's Dictionary defines a promise as a legally binding declaration that gives the person to whom it is made a right to expect or to claim the performance or forbearance of a specified act. Simply put, it gives someone a reason to expect something; especially, ground for expectation of success, improvement, or excellence.

A promise could also be defined as an agreement or covenant. Both terms reemphasize the legal bound between the two parties, chained together by the expectancy of a better future. This is a vital concept to grasp. Due to the nature of agreements or covenants, in order for the contract to be ratified, both sides must fully agree to terms. In times of old, they made blood covenants. When God called Abraham out of his homeland and family, away from all that was familiar to him, He gave Abraham some promises. Not only did God initiate the promises to Abraham, He reminded him in the fifteenth chapter of Genesis of the established covenant. In this exchange, God instructed Abraham to find and kill a dove, heifer, goat, pigeon and ram. After which, Abraham was to cut the ram, goat, heifer and pigeon in half, lay the pieces in two rows, leaving a path through the center [Gen 15:9-10]. In ancient Near Eastern royal land grant treaties, this type of ritual was done to "seal" the promises made. Through this blood covenant, God confirmed the promises he made to Abraham [Gen 12:2-3]. A blood covenant communicated a self-maledictory oath. In essence, by the two parties walking the path between the slaughtered animals, they were saying, "May this be done to me if I do not keep my oath" [Jer 34:18-19]. This type of oath establishes a certain amount of trust between both parties.

Trust is one of the most vital components of any successful relationship, especially in the case of a promise. At any point in time, when promises are not kept, trust is lost. When trust is lost, relationships decay. No matter the size of the promise or length of the relationship, trust is at the core of the fulfillment of the promise. Not only will trust help you remain steadfast on your journey or quest for your promise, while displaying loyalty to the agreed covenant, it helps you stay in

God's favor. In the final portion of Psalms chapter two, verse 12, the psalmist tells us that "Blessed are all they that put their trust in Him" [Ps 2:12c]. Once you are able to completely place your full trust in God, you can now rest in Him and stop trying to do things your way.

Matthew 11:28 "Come to me, all who labor and are heavy laden, and I will give you rest." In order for the promise to come forth, we must take a break from the labor that caused us to become heavy laden, and allow God to place us into a divine rest. A deep sleep for us to pull out of us that which He has already sown into our lives and spirits. There are some of you who are saying they cannot stop the work we are currently engaged in because there are so many who depends on it and us who perform it. Wait! The Lord is saying, place it in my Hands! Many of us have been working out of our flesh and our reserve. It is a good work, but it is not yielding the kind of fruit at the rate of increase God has designed and set forth. This good work can ultimately produce a promise, but it can be delayed for longer than God originally intended for it to be in our lives.

This delay can be caused by several things, but mainly is due to our inability or unwillingness to STOP, LOOK, AND LISTEN! The stopping does not constitute for us to enter a season of inactivity, but to stand still in God [stand still and see the salvation of the Lord]. This moment of stillness grants us the time to reaffirm and remind ourselves of God's character and nature.

Have you ever been so caught up and enamored by the act of working, and not remembered who tasked you to do the work? There have been times in my life when I found myself working on a task and did not recall who assigned it to me. When we do not remember the one who gave us the assignment, it is difficult for us to account for their character or nature. If we are unable to do so, we definitely cannot account or measure the consequences or rewards that are due to us upon completion of the task. It is one thing not to remember your boss, but it is something entirely not to remember God. The various names of God speak of His wide-ranging characteristics. God does not just do good things, but He is goodness! When God charged Moses to return to Egypt and deliver the Israelites, Moses asked what god should he inform the people who has authorized him. God responded by saying, "I AM, that I AM." In other words; whatever and whoever you need God to be for you; whatever characteristic Moses needed to complete the assignment, I AM! When we stop and remind ourselves of God's character, we should become encouraged and excited about what we are doing whom we are doing it for.

Anytime we come to place of rest, we give our minds an opportunity to reflect on the many images and visions we hold in our spirits. During this time, we can evoke the act of gathering one self and reflecting is simply the act of rendering praise unto God for that which He has already done. Why gather and reflect? The gathering is to begin to document all of the conquests and successes witnessed in our lives. Then take a moment to recall the image of the joy you experienced during the last victory. After you have the image fixed in your mind, now you can begin to offer up praises to your Lord. The offering of praise takes our eyes and minds off of the physical realm, the present conditions and state, and places them both in the spiritual. It enables us to rise above the circumstances and begin to "walk by faith and not by sight." Our time of reflection causes us to preach and prophesy to ourselves, proclaiming God's wondrous works and awesome promises, which await us in the near future. It is truly difficult to carry a tremendous burden of negativity and failure when the eyes and mind is constantly drowning in a sea of despair day after day. This should give greater credence for the need to offer censure praise unto the God of heaven and earth, which generates a sweet fragrance in

His nostrils. As we lift up praises to our God, it prompts Him to step into our situation and respond accordingly.

Now that we have stopped and looked, we now must demonstrate the capacity to listen in our resting period. Why is the ability to hear so crucial to obtaining our promise? The art of listening is the act of remaining alert and attentive to what someone is saying, remaining in a position of readiness to respond properly at the right time. One of the most assured ways to hear God is to remain close to Him. In other words, it calls for a heart of worship. It is quite challenging to worship when we are consistently busy with the affairs of life. It is no different than a spouse or child demanding our undivided attended for the purpose of engaging in a fruitful conversation. By engaging in a time of worship, our spirits will soon be replenished, causing us to feel like eagles. In praise, God produces deliverance, but when we engage in worship, God begins to develop our spirits. It is in the position of worship when God can mold and shape us, depositing divine treasures in our hearts that can only come from the throne of God. He speaks to us His enriching thoughts concerning our lives, which unlocks the mysteries that has confounded us years. God-ward worship is the key to our future! It unclogs our spirits and enables us to hear God more clear and concise.

The promise is not always about cars, houses, money, or jobs. Maybe it is deliverance, healing, salvation, hope, comfort or peace. Dependent upon where you are in life, you may need to fix your eyes and attitude on a promise that will bring you into a greater state of being in your time on earth. There are numerous amounts of promises recorded in the Bible, God has designed and stored up for His creation.

Far too often, we become complacent in ourselves believing our dreams and promises are merely fantasies. We relegate ourselves to believe our promises are for other people, another time or we simply give up. The hope of a better and glorious life seemingly begins to evaporate like a drop of water attempting to withstand the hot desert sun. The image of this promise fades from our minds like a haze in the sunset, increasingly becoming more blurred second by second. Never forget, "for everything there is a season and a time for every purpose under heaven."

Often times, God waits for our faith to move us towards Him so He can begin to move our promise towards us. Instead, we find ourselves waiting for God to deliver our promises to us while sitting in a swamp of hopelessness. When we are reluctant to walk by faith and not by our present condition and circumstances, it ties God's hands and delays His response. We must realize that God is drawn to faith. He is attracted to it. The more faith exhibited towards God, the greater the response from God.

Psalms 105:42-45 "For he remembered his holy promise, and Abraham his servant. And he brought forth his people with joy, and his chosen with gladness: And gave them the lands of the heathen: and they inherited the labour of the people; That they might observe his statutes, and keep his laws. Praise ye the Lord."

The amount of faith an individual possesses and is willing to put on display will ultimately decide the release of your promise. Whether you are spiritual or not, your faith in God, your principles, people or even yourself is the determining factor for you receiving the thing(s) you have fixed your hope. The Bible tells us, "faith is the assurance of things hoped for, a conviction of things not seen." [ASV] It is the ability to establish a firm, solid and unyielding foundation designed to sustain and support you while undergoing an arduous process to satisfy an internal appetite of optimism. Faith is what keeps the human spirit from tapping out in life; not giving up on the dreams and goals you have envisioned.

Humans were created to be people of faith. When born, each of us was dealt a measure of faith in our spirit, and through the years, it was nurtured and watered by several different key elements in our lives: *our life experiences, environment, repetitious activity and words, and credible people or sources.* The combination of these four elements makes up the human belief system. This concept is crucial to know and understand, because, if you do not believe, you will achieve that which you are seeking. In essence, your faith cannot be activated until you truly believe. It is a prerequisite for igniting the progress towards the reception of your promise.

The first element of the human belief system is our life experience, and it is the most impactful element of the four mentioned. It is the experiences in life that causes us to hold true to the events in life that will shape our beliefs, whether consciously or unconsciously. There are three kinds of life experiences: natural, soulish and spiritual. Each experience is distinct in its own right, providing a necessary, impactful occurrence in our lives that gives utterance to belief.

A natural experience is no more than you personally encountering or witnessing an event. For example; in football, when the quarterback calls a pass play, it is the responsibility for each receiver to run their routes properly with maximum effort to ensure the quarterback has a clear path to get the receiver the ball. If the receiver leaves the huddle not believing in the play, or does not believe the quarterback can or will get him the ball, it is highly probable the ball will not be thrown his way. The receiver's lack of belief in the play or the quarterback could have cost the team a first down, a touchdown, or even a win. The play calls for more than just two or three players to be synchronized in their belief, and trust each other to fulfill the given assignments on each specific play. Actually, there are actually eleven players on offense that have eleven distinct assignments on a given play. If the players don't believe in the play or their teammates, they are less likely to be disciplined in the various techniques and awareness of executing the play properly against their opponent. It is things like this that causes one to lose focus and demonstrate a lack of attentiveness, which could result in the entire game plan veering off course. Each of the eleven players must believe in the play and in each other to maximize the results and success of the play, but it all starts with their belief. For a sports team, their belief in each other and the coach's system begins in training camp. The players must be able to see it in operation. Once they see it, and can see themselves in it, they will begin to believe and operate at another level!

A soulish experience occurs in the soul of a man. It takes an individual on a journey and simulates an experience in their mind that makes them feel or believe the encounter was real. Have you ever had a dream and felt it was so real that you were awakened from your sleep? In doing so, your mind simulates a real life experience to the degree you believe your dream was actually your reality. This type of experience occurs in the soul and initiates the genesis of belief in this very occurrence.

The third life experience that makes a significant impact on a human's life and belief system is the spiritual experience. This kind of experience occurs in the life of an individual who receives a life-like vision from God. This vision or occurrence is so real that it compels and propels the individual to carry out the assignment or mission communicated through the vision. A good example of this was Ezekiel in the valley of dry bones and it compelled him to go forth and speak the word of God, or even the Apostle John who received a holy vision on the Island of Patmos and prompted him to write the book of Revelation. These men and their accounts are just two examples of the overwhelming impact the spirit realm has on our lives and our belief systems.

It is difficult for a man or woman to believe and have faith in something they cannot touch, or let alone see. Like Thomas, the disciple infamously known as "doubting Thomas." I wonder how Thomas actually feels about everyone calling him a doubter. Thomas merely expressed his thoughts concerning the testimony of his brothers. What if Andrew or Peter was not there when Jesus returned, could they have not felt the same way? Would you have believed their story? Especially since these were the same men who fled after they took Jesus captive. These were things occurring in their lives that never happened before; it was unheard of; beyond belief. Now, you're telling me [Thomas] that you want me to believe that the same man, who was just beat to a bloody pulp, crucified on a tree and buried three days prior, is walking around as if nothing ever happened. In those days, there were no holograms and experimental cloning by the scientist. So, Thomas was saying that he had to see this for himself! He had to fix his eyes on Jesus, and place his hands on him to balance their claim and validate his belief, confidence or faith in the very words that Jesus spoke concerning the promise of His resurrection.

In John chapter 20, the Apostle John gives an account of the resurrected Christ and the unbelieving Thomas. He wanted to see! This means that all of the teachings and words Jesus shared with Thomas over the three years of ministry did not bring him to a place of assurance pertaining to Jesus' resurrection. Thomas, with his human mind, could not fathom how such a thing could occur. In his mind, he had no image or example of this every existing. He had no mental point of reference for this life experience, thus paralyzing his belief in the others disciples life experience. This seriously challenged Thomas' belief system, but it also challenges others. Without the mental reference, people lacking faith in certain areas of their lives, the human mind requires a previous experience.

Abraham is another example of someone whose belief system was challenged. Yes, Abraham is known as the "father of faith." Yes, Abraham demonstrated great faith and obedience to leave his country and family behind to travel to a foreign land at the command of God. Abraham responded to God with devout obedience and worship, following His every command, but when it came to God blessing Abraham with a child, his faith was shaken.

Gen 15:1-6 "After these things the word of Jehovah came unto Abram [Abraham] in a vision, saying, Fear not, Abram [Abraham]: I am thy shield, and thy exceeding great reward. And Abram [Abraham] said, O Lord Jehovah, what wilt thou give me, seeing I go childless, and he that shall be possessor of my house is Eliezer of Damascus? And Abram [Abraham] said, Behold, to me thou hast given no seed: and, lo, one born in my house is mine heir. And, behold, the word of Jehovah came unto him, saying, This man shall not be thine heir; But he that shall come forth out of thine own bowels shall be thine heir. And he brought him forth abroad, and said, Look now toward heaven, and number the stars, if thou be able to number them: and he said unto him, So shall thy seed be. And he believed in Jehovah; and he reckoned it to him for righteousness.

In this passage, God begins this dialogue with Abraham saying "fear not." Anytime God tells you not to fear, means that you are not operating in faith; fear is the opposite of faith. This dialogue Abraham has with God occurred in a vision. Whether it was a day vision or night vision, God understood that Abraham needed a mental picture of the promise God made with him. This vision given to Abraham by God was the key to unlocking Abraham's faith in God, solidifying the very foundation that he would walk out the remainder of his life in covenant with God. I believe every decision Abraham made from that point was predicated on the image God unveiled to him through the vision. Once Abraham saw the vision, the Bible says, *"And he believed in Jehovah."* The Scripture shows us that Abraham, "father of faith," did not believe God concerning the promise of an heir until it was shown to him.

God deals and responds to us according to our faith. Our faith hinges on the things that we are able to attribute to an image, example or model. Could this be the reason why you have yet to accomplish your dream? You cannot see it. You have not been able to break through the barriers of your mind to dream of a better version of your life. Often times, this is caused by a dry and desolate environment. This is the second factor in our belief system is determined by our environment. When our environments have been impoverished and lacking fertile examples to successful lives on a consistent basis, it does not generate a positive attitude towards a bright and prosperous future for oneself. It is quite difficult for one to see him or her attaining a promise when no one in their environment shows any sign of promise. For example, when majority of your peers are being murdered, incarcerated or having children all while in their teenage years, your environment is hindering your belief system. It becomes more and more difficult by the day for someone living in this environment to believe they can accomplish or become anything more than they see on a daily basis in their environment. Likewise, as people are exposed to more in life and are able to others operating in the same things they desire for themselves. Whether the environment is negative or positive, it makes a strong impact on the lives of those engulfed in it.

The other two elements derive from repetitious activity and words, and credible people and sources. It is believed these two elements may have more impact on today's society by way of the media than the impact of life experiences. The marketing and advertising industry has made billions of dollars in sales through the years by understanding the principle of repetition and the need for credible people and sources to deliver a consistent message. Television advertisers understand that when they play the same programs repetitively using actors and actresses you like and consider credible sources to impact your belief system. By leveraging this methodology, the advertisers now impose their will on the mental intellect of the viewers, driving them to a place to desire and act on the images and messages communicated through the various mediums.

In the same manner, when we apply this same principle to our lives in a positive way, we should reap an abundance of prosperous results.

Psalms 1:1-3 "Blessed is the man that walketh not in the counsel of the wicked, Nor standeth in the way of sinners, Nor sitteth in the seat of scoffers: But his delight is in the law of Jehovah; And on his law doth he meditate day and night. And he shall be like a tree planted by the streams of water, That bringeth forth its fruit in its season, Whose leaf also doth not wither; And whatsoever he doeth shall prosper."

This is telling us the expected outcome of an individual who consciously decides to take good counsel, and meditate on the law of the Lord day and night. The one who meditates on the law of the Lord day and night shall be like a planted tree by the streams of water. The Hebrew word used for meditate is the same Hebrew word used in the Bible for imagination. In order words, as you meditate or imagine day and night on the law of the Lord, you will be producing your own mental video of your expected end, possessing your promise. You must be willing and able to make your own motion picture of you living your life with your promise so you can begin doing the necessary things to walk it out.

───────── ○ ● ○ ─────────

There are far too many people who have become subconsciously dependent upon people they have no Earthly business being dependent upon.

───────── ○ ● ○ ─────────

You must be able to attach your faith in God to the image of your promise that which you hope to manifest. This concept of hope gives birth to a stream of creative thoughts to produce an even flow of energy to manufacture your expected outcome. Therefore, faith must not only remain as a verb in our lives, it must become a noun. It must become as a person, place or thing, that we may become bound and married our your future; our wonderful promise. When you allow for your faith to transpose from not just working but being, the image of you existing in your promise will become much more evident.

When you are able to get a vision of yourself with your promise, you will develop an attitude of preparation. The mere glimpse of an image of yourself with your promise will birth an overwhelming excitement in your spirit. In turn, this will drive you to do some things others may deem foolish and wasteful. I am talking about a husband and wife who believe God for children purchasing a crib, basinett, diapers, a play pen and the works before they ever receive confirmation of a pregnancy. Maybe you are a man believing God for the promise of a wife, and you already purchased the engagement ring. Only faith in the vision of your promise, and faith in the Promisor can drive someone to prepare a structure for something that has yet to make its estimated time of arrival known.

This attitude of preparation is a sheer explosion of great faith! Your faith will cause you to leap while others are still trying to walk. Every time you pass something that coincides with your promise, you are driven to connect with it, knowing it is a necessary component to support the very thing promise being pulled into your sphere. This attitude is corralled by the wisdom of the Holy Spirit, leading and guiding you in your every move and decision. It is pertinent for you not to allow your emotions to overtake you, but remaining obedient to the Holy Spirit for the blessings of the Lord to overtake you.

PREPARATION EMULATES GOD

John 14:1-3 "Let not your heart be troubled: believe in God, believe also in me. In my Father's house are many mansions; if it were not so, I would have told you; for I go to prepare a place for you. And if I go and prepare a place for you, I

come again, and will receive you unto myself; that where I
am, there ye may be also. [ASV]

What did Jesus say? Jesus has to go to his Father's house to prepare a place for us? In this passage, Jesus began speaking to the disciples in an attempt to increase their faith in Him (the Messiah) and Father God. Jesus now introduces Himself as the ultimate preparer. In some of His last moments of on earth, He began to speak to His leaders in training about a place that He is going to prepare for those who will come after Him, for all those who choose to believe in Him. He clearly tells the disciples that He is *"going to prepare a place"*, in another translation, He says, He is going to *"get your room ready."* If Jesus believes it is important for Him to prepare His Father's house for us, which has many mansions or rooms, how much more important is it for us to learn to prepare? How much more should we be concerned about preparing our house for the Father and many gifts He brings? Jesus felt it necessary to explain that if He prepares this place for us, He will return to take us to the very place He prepared and will remain with us in this place. He never mentioned the exact process or tasks He needed to complete in order to make ready a place for us in His Father's house, but we do know some of the things Jesus did prior to ascending to heaven. What we do know is that prior to His ascension, He "descended into the lower part of the earth." [Eph 6:10]

Jesus' preparation of the Father's mansion for us was predicated on descending into the lower parts of the earth to take the keys of death and of Hades from the enemy. The keys He took back represent authority, dominion and power previously lost by Adam in the garden. The keys represent the access and ability we need to gain admission to our original purpose and destinies in this earth.

Consider when God created the earth and Adam. He prepared the earth to receive a man to have dominion and subdue every living creature upon the face of the earth. God is a God of preparation. There was nothing that needed to be created for the man after God created him; everything he needed, God created for him with an ability to produce out of himself any additional desires. The act of creating in advance, or preplanning is a characteristic of God. In Genesis, it lays out the order of creation; how God created the heavens and the earth. It provides great insight on how the earth was prepared for man prior to his arrival. It gives us a clear depiction of God's ability and wisdom to prepare things prior to releasing the ultimate promise. Before Adam was mentioned or even created, God had already prepared for him a source of nourishment, shelter, occupation, and creatures to oversee. To go even further, God created the water before He created the fish. He created the herbs and blades of grass prior to establishing any livestock in the earth. God did this; He prepared something for living creatures prior to placing them in an atmosphere of dwelling in the earth. If God created us in His image and likeness, and He prepared a world to receive us as we receive it, how much more important is it for us to learn to prepare for the things He desires to give us? How much more successful would you be if you begin to prepare your life to receive your dreams and goals?

To become like Christ, to be attain the image and likeness of God in the earth, we must learn to prepare. Preparation is a characteristic of God. It is one of the first characteristics of God the Bible illustrates so plainly to us during the creation process. God took the time to do things in advanced as He molded and shaped every aspect of this world to ensure it was ready for man's occupancy. This reaffirms the very nature of God and His abilities as an all-knowing and encompassing architect, and the wisdom to strategize and foresee the end of a thing from its beginning. These are the kinds of character traits we should desire with all our hearts to display and emulate.

To accomplish the type of success both God and you desire to achieve in your life, these attributes are vital to your being. You need wisdom God to know what to do, when to do it, the specific place the perform it, and understand why you are doing it. The characteristic of insight to perceive things as you encounter them, and the attribute of foresight to see ahead of your present situations and employ the necessary strategies to manifest the expected end in line with God's will. Last but not least, you need to maintain an attitude and spirit of obedience. This will help you remain humble, and synchronized with God as He is moving and speaking. Each trait is crucial to finishing your race with the prize you have so sought after.

PREPARATION DEVELOPS AND REQUIRES DISCIPLINE

King Solomon, the son of King David, known as the wisest man to walk the face of the earth, as well as one of the most foolish men. History tells us that when he succeeded his father as king of Israel, God granted him with unsurpassed wisdom to lead the nation of Israel. Ironically, the man who sought wisdom to lead a nation later disobeyed the commandments and ordinances of the very God he honored and pleased with his humble request. King Solomon could have requested anything from God, but he chose wisely, demonstrating his love for the people and most of all, his love for God.

Often times, we as people really do not need someone to give us the things we want, but rather the requirement of wisdom to know and understand how to acquire them ourselves. If you never teach a man to fish, they will always be dependent upon the one who continues to give them fish. It is important for us to teach the next generation, as well as the present, how to fish for the things their heart desires. There are far too many people who have become subconsciously dependent upon people they have no earthly business being dependent upon them for anything. To be honest, they one you may find yourself heavily dependent upon is acquiring their resources from another source, thereby making them continue an exhausting facade as they remain dependent upon someone else in order that you will continue to come to them for as a source for food. This is a vicious cycle. If you have found yourself in this type of relationship, ask God to intervene, break the cycle and become your source for sustainment, in the mighty name of Jesus!

While King Solomon accumulated much wealth and status as king of Israel during his reign, yet he later realized he lacked discipline in the things of God. During his realization, he shares many of the lessons learned and wisdom nuggets deposited in him through his years of reign as king. He is attributed to providing the world with some of the most insightful documented teachings in the history of mankind. The king is credited with writing much of the book of Proverbs, the Song of Solomon, the book of Ecclesiastes, and two psalms.

In these writings, we find a statement in the book of Proverbs chapter 30 where he makes a profound statement about four of the littlest of creatures on the face of the earth, but "they are exceeding wise." Following this statement, the first creature mentioned is the ant. This is what King Solomon tells us in Proverbs about the ant:

Proverbs 30:25 say, "The ants are a people not strong, yet they prepare their meat in the summer."

The ant derives from the Formicate family, which the bees and wasps also belong. The ant is known to be the most intelligent species of insects with approximately 250,000 brain cells, and have an average life span of 45-60 days. It is said that ants are one of the most successful groups of insects in the animal kingdom. They are one of the most socially adept species known on earth and form highly organized colonies that often consist of thousands to millions of ants. According to historical records, ants were farming long before humans. The fungus farm ant began their agricultural undertakings about 50 million years prior to mankind's farming exploits. With the ant being a very small creature that no we as humans could really care less about until they begin to infiltrate our space, they have colonized almost every landmass on earth. Whether we find them in the yard, on the porch, or even as they find their way into our homes, we rarely give them any sorts of attention.

Now, the wisest man known to man tells us that the ant is "exceeding wise." This is very strong statement for an insect, especially when he begins his description of the ant as lacking strength. The question we should pose is what makes the ant wise. Or maybe we should ask what does the writer see in the ant that causes him to see wisdom, yet he does not see it in other things as a whole. What is the writer trying to get us to see in the ant that we should be replicate in our lives?

First, the text illustrates the characteristic and mentality of the ant. The ant is preparing for winter in the summer! The writer describes the ant as a people who knows how to prepare for that which is coming during a season and a time with no evidence of its existence. The writer is presenting the ant as a people who possess the wherewithal to focus on the promise of that which is to come, rather than wasting time enjoying its present conditions. The ant has relinquished the past failures and conquests, but has set its sights on that which it longs to have and to hold. The ant is married to its future, and every ounce of energy is geared towards it. There will be no wasted energy on frivolous fantasies and notions of lazing around in the sun during the summer months. The ant knows and understands that winter is coming and it is time to prepare. The ant knows and understands that in order to be prepared, it has to get to work.

Proverbs 6:6-9 "Go to the ant, thou sluggard; consider her ways, and be wise: which having no guide, overseer, or ruler, provideth her meat in the summer, and gathereth her food in the harvest. How long wilt thou sleep, O sluggard? When wilt thou arise out of thy sleep? Yet a little sleep, a little slumber, a little folding of the hands to sleep: so shall thy poverty come as one that travelleth, and thy want as an armed man."

The ant has a good work ethic. God designed man with the same characteristics He instilled in the ant, the instincts and desire to work. The first thing God gave Adam, before he received a woman to be by his side, he received a job. Adam learned how to work and produce with his hands before he learned to announce and pronounce a creature's identity. Employment was assigned to his hands prior to him exercising the ability and authority of his words. Often times, we allow our words to get so far ahead of our works. Remember, "Faith without works is dead!" You show me a man with great faith, and I'll show you a man with great works. If all we need is a grain of faith to help us move, then we should immediately begin working toward our promise. If the promise is a home or vehicle, begin working to prepare your credit. If the promise is a spouse, prepare your home and go buy the rings. If your promise is your calling or purpose, you should begin working to prepare your life. Anything worth having is worth preparing for.

The ant provides an example of a species much smaller than you, with far less intellectual capacity, possessing an abundance of belief and tenacity in their ability to not only see what they want but to bear the weight of it. Not only can the ant carry 100 times its weight, but also does so to gather its treasure during a season of harvest and store it in preparation for a predetermined future. The ant not only observes the opportunity, but also assesses and seizes it as a prey to conquer. In like manner, begin to seek opportunities to seize the moments to prepare for that which is to come. Grab a hold of it in your season of harvest, placing it in your reserve for the time ahead.

Preparation takes part in every day of our lives. Daily, we are preparing food, preparing for work, preparing for class, preparing to speak, preparing to entertain, holidays, etc. Amazing enough, all of these things seem to warrant so much attention and consideration. They keep us up at all times of the night, pacing the floor over what to wear, what to do, what and how to phrase comments, the kinds of decorations for a particular event or occasion. Most assuredly each of these garner the necessary dedication, but what about the amount of devotion required to benefit the realization of your promise?

Not only are we to work, but also we must be diligent in our preparation. Remember, God is "a rewarder of them who diligently seek him." Newton's Law of Motion reminds us "every object in a state of uniform motion tends to remain in that state of motion unless an external force is applied to it." This constant motion helps us picture the necessary consistency required by you to achieve your ultimate prize. Preparation is to be performed deliberately and meticulously. The uniformity of the motion we should strive to exemplify is an accurate and precise act of preparation. Like a surgeon, there are no wasted motions or strokes of the scalpel; every action in the operating room has a succinct plan and purpose for an expected end.

—————— ○ ● ○ ——————

The mere glimpse of an image of yourself with your promise will birth an overwhelming excitement in your spirit.

—————— ○ ● ○ ——————

When God created the world in six days, He took the time to rest on the seventh day. If God was willing to put forth the work to prepare a world for us during the six days of creation, we should be willing to labor for that which He desires to release into our lives. This work that I am speaking of is not a curse, but the attitude we have towards the work ignites the curse. We as people must be willing to partner with God to produce in the earth. As the old adage goes, "nothing in, nothing out." Whether it is an attitude of unbelief, unenthusiastic or unwillingness, you begin to curse the very thing you say you believe God to produce in your life. This negative attitude towards working towards your promise builds an invisible wall between you, God and your promise.

The ant is determined to achieve its goal. Unfortunately, every human being can learn this lesson from the ant. Far too often we give up while in pursuit of dreams and goals. The sad truth of the matter is that we don't give up on God, or the thing, but rather we give up on ourselves. The things we are seeking after never move, but because of our lack of confidence in our ability to accomplish the mission, many of us would rather give up in the midst of the race. We have a tendency to take our hands off of the things and place them on our hips or behind our backs as a sign of exhaustion, and we are waving the white flag.

When you find yourself in that kind of situation, remember the ant. As the ant is on the trail seeking for food in preparation for winter, they resist every obstacle that may present itself to them while on their mission. You have to declare in the atmosphere "No weapon formed against you shall prosper" [Isaiah 54:17]. As they press towards their goal, they continue their forward progress and fight. The fight is not always physical, but often times its mental. They are not concerned with the enemy and his vices, but are vigilant in their pursuit of their goal. The ant is not even enamored by the size of the thing they desire to grab. They simply devise a plan, latch hold, and begin to pull it back their destination. As previously stated, the ant has the ability to carry 100 times its own body weight. So, regardless of the size of the obstacle that confronts the ant, it will not stop until it achieves its goal.

We must take on the mentality of the ant of not allowing yourself to quit. You must declare "Quitting is not an option for me!" You must begin to prepare yourself for that which is ahead of you; begin to move. Purposeful movement is your friend. You must move with the assurance knowing that you have a date with destiny, and every act of preparation draws you closer to securing its place in your life. Failure is not an option, and quitting is not your portion. Just know that every time you exercise your faith, you are pulling your predestined promises into sphere of existence. Regardless of how big the promise may be, grab hold of it and begin to pull it in through strategic, diligent preparation.

The ant is focused. The ant sets its eyes on the winter in the season of summer. The atmosphere and climate does not sway the focus of the ant. Despite how hot it may be in the region the ant finds itself during the summer months, the ant only sees itself surrounded by the images snow. The ant only sees winter elements in its eyes, which further exasperates the need for preparation activities to take priority in its life. The shadows of the past are no longer evident, and the present is rendered powerless of any distractions. This causes the mind to remain solely concentrated on the vision of itself living abundantly in its place of promise.

The text not only tells us what the ant does, but when he does it. The ant is like a focused champion training for another battle. During the champion's time of training, whether it is weeks or months, all types of diverse distractions confront him. Regardless of the distraction, the champion must remain focused in order to properly prepare for his opponent. He cannot or must not take his training lightly, because by doing so, he is disrespecting his opponent. In fact, the champion is so focused in his preparation, that he establishes training sessions in atmospheric conditions that closely resemble the very environment he expects to conquer his next opponent. He does this for the sole purpose of teaching himself to maintain his focus in similar conditions so he can avoid the many distractions that will attempt to delay or deny him from his expected promise; whether knowingly or unknowingly.

Similarly, Jesus provides us the ultimate example of someone who remained focus on his promise despite his circumstances. In Hebrews 12:2, the writer tells us "looking unto Jesus the author and finisher of our faith…" gives us a perfect example of how we must not allow harmful words and dry situations. Despite the persecution, rejection, and all the hate-filled words spoken to and about Him, Jesus continued to press forward to complete His assignment. He remained focused to deliver the promise to all mankind, just as we must remain focused on God, our Heavenly Father. Jesus knew His outcome. He understood and knew that as longs as He remained focused and did not quit, He could become the perfect sacrifice for mankind.

He remained focused by "praying without ceasing." Jesus remained in constant communication with the Heavenly Father. This communication did not occur in public, but rather privately on a daily basis. Jesus was not praying with His friends, the disciples, about the plans and thoughts of God concerning life. Every time the Bible mentioned Jesus in prayer, it typically began with, "He rose early

When we look, we really should be observing with our spiritual eyes. The Apostle Paul said it like this, *"the eyes of your understanding being enlightened"* [Eph 1:18]. As we look, it grants us the time and opportunity to gather ourselves and reflect on the past victories and where God has placed us in this season. It is common for us to become fixed on our present circumstances and situations, but we remain focused on the Promisor and not the promise. This allows us to gain the confidence to press forward despite the circumstances by stop reacting to the circumstances and situations we see everyday, and begin preparing the appropriate responses to change the atmosphere that will order each day, downloading God's divine will for your life. It is imperative for us to realize and come to understand that the images we capture with our eyes can poison our minds with discouragement and doubt, causing us to simply react negatively with fatal words and actions.

The ant understands and trusts sound principles. Principles are in every phase and aspect of the human life. There are principles for agriculture, chemistry, biology, botany, business, money, physics, spiritual and stewardship are just few that we recognize and practice regularly. A principle could be a fundamental truth that serves as your system of belief for your reasoning, a scientific theorem or law with multiple special applications, or just your basis for something. Dependent upon the type of principle you decide to employ, it could produce a variety of results. However, the kind of principle we are speaking of is the fundamental truth or proposition that serves our lives as the ground which we stand with our unyielding belief and behavior towards things.

Now, this type of principle is can produce some bountiful results if you choose the correct principle and understand how to properly apply it to your life. Possessing a strong foundational, unwavering belief sets you up for extraordinary things to occur in that area of your life when you successfully apply the principle. Regardless of the season or conditions, the principle must consistently be at work in your life. If the principle becomes employed at any time, it can result in chaos or create an imbalance. This is what occurs when the principle of saving is not in operation in your life. Despite the amount of money you make, the lack of saving presents issues for long term planning. It becomes quite difficult to see your prosperous future when so many things you purchased unnecessarily cloud your present day.

The ant employs one simple principle, plan ahead and prepare. The ability to plan ahead and prepare means that you already know, understand and assured of a goal or destination in mind. The adoption of this principle grants the ability and capacity to obtain a constant attitude of preparation. It also lends a vivid image of oneself in existing in your destination or goal, which then allows you the ability to deduce the necessary resources needed to secure this expected future. Your sights are

now firmly planted in what lies ahead, with the unimpaired confidence that you will get to a place called there!

When you are able to get a vision of yourself with your promise, you will develop an attitude of preparation. The mere glimpse of an image of yourself with your promise will birth an overwhelming excitement in your spirit. In turn, this will drive you to do some things others may deem foolish and wasteful. I am talking about the husband and wife who are believing God for children going to purchase a crib, basinett, diapers, a play pen and the works before they ever take the pregnancy test. Maybe you are a man believing God for the promise of a wife, and you already purchased the engagement ring. Only faith in the vision of your promise, and faith in the Promisor can drive someone to prepare a structure for something that has yet to make its estimated time of arrival known.

This attitude of preparation is a shear explosion of great faith! Your faith will cause you to leap while others are trying to walk. Every time you pass something that coincides with your promise, you are driven to acquire it, knowing it is a necessary component to support the very thing promise being pulled into my sphere. This attitude is corralled by the wisdom of the Holy Spirit, leading and guiding you in your every move and decision. It is pertinent for you not to allow your emotions to overtake you, but remaining obedient to the Holy Spirit for the blessings of the Lord to overtake you.

Thankfully, the ant was able to clearly see its future. The ant had a fixed heart and a made up mind that it was willing and able to wait. The ant believes that if it makes the necessary provisions through its preparations, it would have the necessary resources when it arrives in the winter season. This is the principle of patience operating in the life of the ant. This patience is not stagnate or infertile, but it is patience with aggression. The ant aggressively seeks after food and stores it away for a time yet to come. The ant identified the resources necessary for its future; for the place it saw and believed it would be in an upcoming season. The audacity of the ant to think it can successfully acquire resources that had little to no value for its life today, but position them in its life for a later date when its value would have appreciated.

It is amazing how the ant is able to grab a hold of the things necessary to secure its future, while remaining in his today, yet forgetting about the past concerns. To properly emulate the ant, you must first seize the attitude and mentality of someone who understands what promises are ahead, and demonstrate the willingness to prepare yourself while patiently waiting for your future to become your present. Do not give way to doubt, delays or distractions, but keep your eyes on the prize. Attitude it everything! It is the fiber you eat in the morning for breakfast as you climb out of bed. Your attitude is the snack you enjoy while commuting to work, fighting your way through traffic. It is the delicious and ever succulent meal you partake during your afternoon lunch, amid the chaotic and sometimes challenging working environment. Your attitude is your dinner or supper that satisfies your appetite at the end of your day, ensuring you have supplemented your body as best as possible with the necessary nutrients and proteins. The attitude you adorn your life with daily has significant impact on whether you are drawing closer to receiving your promise, or pushing yourself in a direction opposite of a much desired and anticipated dream.

The plan ahead and prepare principle keeps you aligned and focused. It actually keeps you in the race. When it seems as if things around you are falling apart, you can always fall back on your plans and preparations and you should find some sort of comfort about the path you are currently traveling. The plans and preparations can aid in providing a barometer for your current position, while seeking God for direction and the next step or strategy to leverage.

To successfully work this principle, you must seek out new experiences and explore new territories. You cannot merely keep doing the same thing, and going to the same places expecting for something new and miraculous to occur in your life. As you seek out these new experiences, you will learn from your adversities. Until pressure is applied to the nut, it is impossible to extract all of the precious oil it holds on the inside. Every adversity presents a new learning opportunity, as well as gauging your maturation on how to handle the difficult times. Now that you have sought out new things and embraced your adversities as teaching curriculums, you now put your must stay ready. I remember my high school coach always reminding the team that if you stay ready, you will never have to get ready. When you remain prepared, you will never find yourself in a situation when you are caught by surprise. If your desire is to build or grow your business and you are seeking that one big opportunity, you must always be prepared to have your elevator speech ready at a moment's notice. You may be a woman seeking for a husband; you should always leave your home beautified, adorned with purpose and virtue, with the expectation of your Boaz finding you gleaning in the field.

Regardless of your desired promise, you must plan ahead and prepare yourself mentally and physically to encounter it and a pull it into your life. It is absolutely imperative that you seize every moment to work this principle in your life, home, business, ministry or any other phase of your being. You must leave no stone unturned as you work this principle to the extent it now becomes the norm. As you are able to successfully employ and apply this rule to your life, it will become easy for you to step into opportunities divinely set aside and formed for your life.

PREPARATION ESTABLISHES STRUCTURE

The necessity of preparing your life before you receive your promise can be found in the concept of knowing that preparation helps build a structure to house it once it arrives. To what level will you be able to enjoy your promise and live life the in the manner which God intended f you are not prepared to handle it. Notice I did not say you lack the ability or capacity to keep, but you are not prepared to deal with the various responsibilities that come with it. Before a house can be decorated and furnished, it first must be built, and prior to building the house, the foundation must be laid. If you thought the foundation was the first thing in the building process, you may want to identify the location or lot for the house to sit. Yet, in order to find the right lot to sufficiently accommodate this home, you would require blueprints for the house.

The blueprints are designed and approved by a licensed architect who has knowledge and experience with county codes, weight distribution and the kind of material and resources needed to make this drawing an actual reality. The architect takes into consideration the atmosphere and climates the home will be built, ensuring proper insulation and cooling is achieved. For instance, if you have ever been to Arizona or in the California desert, the homes are designed and built vastly different from those on the east coast. They use different wood and different shingles. As a matter of fact, most the homes I saw did not use siding or brick. As an architect, these are things you must know and be familiar with when preparing to build homes. If not, frankly you probably will need to find another career because your ability to execute insight and foresight for the homes you design will not yield in many sells.

Ironically, Jesus told a story about two architects who each built a house. Now, one of the architects displayed wisdom, insight and foresight, while the other seemed to have lacked at least two of the three. While one architect possessed the ability to build a home that was prepared for any storms it may face, the other builder gave the impression that he was only concerned with the superficial qualities of the home. Yes, I know that huge chandelier in foyer and dining room seems like a must have, and the heated marble floors would look and feel great under your bare feet late at night or early in the morning making that much needed trip to the refrigerator. Yet, it may not be too helpful when your home is being hit with winds with speed of more that 50 mph. Let's take a look at the story.

Matthew 7:24-26 "Therefore whosoever heareth these sayings of mine, and doeth them, I will liken him unto a wise man, which built his house upon a rock: And the rain descended, and the floods came, and the winds blew, and beat upon that house; and it fell not: for it was founded upon a rock. And every one that heareth these sayings of mine, and doeth them not, shall be likened unto a foolish man, which built his house upon the sand: And the rain descended, and the floods came, and the winds blew, and beat upon that house; and it fell: and great was the fall of it. "

The first man, Jesus describes him as wise because he "built his house upon a rock." Obviously, the man already had his blueprint design for his home. Now, he had to know and understand the atmosphere or elements in which his home would to reside. After surveying the land, he determined the exact position for the home. In his surveys, he determined where some of the biggest and strongest rocks that could hold his home safely and securely. Then he began to dig. He dug deep until hit a rock, which he set as the foundation for his house. The man was able to secure a solid, unmovable fixture that would now become a place of strength for his. This fixed object would help provide the assurance and security his home required to ward off the various storms that would come his way in the changing of seasons.

To accomplish each of these feats, and properly prepare to build his dream home that would withstand the tests of time, the wise builder had to exhibit insight, foresight and wisdom. He researched and planned every aspect of the home, making sure he knew the best woods and materials for the inner and outer walls, even down to the smallest of details considering the nails and screws were ideally suited to hold strong in the surrounding climate. With all of the attention to details he gave himself to, he spent the most time dedicated to ensuring the foundation was right. This man was prepared to build his home.

Unlike the first, Jesus described the second builder as a foolish man. This man, a brilliant architect and constructor in his own right, yet his plans and strategy for building his home were a bit ill considered. The depiction of this man's house was that he built it upon sand, upon a foundation that was virtually unable to stabilize the infrastructure of the house. The reason for the man choosing this location and foundation is unknown, other than the fact that Jesus called him a foolish man. In other words, he did not take the time to consider the future and the possible elements and storms the home would have to endure. He may have been misinformed, did not seek the assistance of the right people, or any at all for that fact. Maybe he merely desired to have a beautiful, beach front home, overlooking the waters with the ability to see the glorious sunrise and sunset clear across the horizon. Who knows, he could have just spent most of his time planning the type of hardwood floors he needed, or the dimensions of the master bedroom suite, and ensuring he had finest and most elegant designs money can buy. With all of that stated, he simply did not truly prepare for his dream home to be able to stand through the tests and trials from season to season. The foundation which he placed his home could not powerless to bear the weight, tightly secure its position as the house begin to settle, and it was unable to stand firm amidst of the rain, floods and winds that would constantly beat at its door.

──────── o ● o ────────

Only faith in the vision of your promise, and faith in the Promisor can drive someone to prepare a structure for something that has yet to make its estimated time of arrival known.

──────── o ● o ────────

The right kind of preparation always leads you low. Low in reputation, yet keeping an ascending perspective. In other words, matters not if you have the biggest and most beautiful home in the county if it is unable to protect you and your family during times of storms. The most important component of a house is its foundation. As a matter of fact, it is the strongest portion of the home, probably because it is being supported by the foundation God created. The foundation is the structure always fashioned below the ground. This is to increase or enhance the lateral stability of the structure, and designed to provide a firm and level surface for transmitting the load of the home to the earth. Plainly put, the foundation is designed to keep your house from sinking and sliding away.

Now, the difference between the two building engineers is clear. One focused on beauty and the present, the other focused on preservation and the future. The wise builder's preparation in solidifying the right kind of structure for his home, a foundation capable to weather the rain, floods, winds and adversities of life, gave way to securing his promise of home for his future generations. Due to his ability to foresee past his present circumstances, and prepare a foundation for his home, he could rest easy knowing that his family had a safe haven to run in from the storm. Because of wisdom, the builder could firmly declare that his promise has a structure to hold it.

It takes wisdom to duplicate the actions of the wise builder. It requires insight and foresight to discount your present day realities and start preparing for your next day actualities. You must know, be firmly fixed in your heart and your mind that the images you see with your natural eyes are not representative of the vision God deposited in your heart of an expected future. Begin to plan for your promise. Begin to prepare for your promise. Ensure your promise has a firm, strong foundation that will secure and hold it during times of difficulties and storms. You must be focused in your preparation for this promise.

Be like the wise builder; do the necessary research to find the right place with the biggest and strongest rock and make it your foundation for your promise. That foundation that you are searching for is a specific word from the Lord. Search the scriptures, find a Word that is handcrafted for you and the promise God has given you, and then make that very scripture your foundation. Write it on post-it notes and stick it on your mirrors, pin it to your office wall and do not just read it everyday, but declare it aloud into the atmosphere. Make it become a part of your daily diet. When doubt and discouragement comes, because you have a foundation, which your hope is built upon, you can shift the load to your Word.

Storms come in various forms, shapes and sizes. There are windstorms, rainstorms, sand storms and even hailstorms. Despite the variety of storms, you must know without any reservations that your foundation has secured your promise. Because of the amount of time invested in your preparations, and the confidence in the One you have invested, it offers the necessary assurance to proceed with the remainder of your building plans.

Until the foundation is tested and inspected, all construction of the house has to cease. The foundation must be validated to know it is trusted to support everything that will be placed on it. Therefore, the Word you choose as the foundation for your promise must be tested. It must be proved in your life to ensure you will not sink when as feels as the ground is moving all around you, and the waves of life begin to beat up against you. You can run back to the Word that gives you strength and declare that God is sovereign; He cannot lie and never fails. If God promised it, He shall deliver it.

Understand this point, this why you must use the word of God as a foundation for your promise. I heard Dr. Myles Munroe share this awesome revelation while teaching some time ago. He said, "God is as sovereign as His word. God is limited by His word, and God will never violate His word." So, God forever lives to complete His word. Psalms 138:8 assure us that "The Lord will perfect that which concerns me." God desires to see you whole, living in your promises throughout your generations. If you have submitted your life to Christ, and declared that He is Lord over your life, God has to do it for you; His name and reputation is on the line. That is why God is limited by His word, because He cannot violate His word. When a king does not protect and care for his citizens, his kingdom loses its value and citizens will defame his name. Since God is King of kings, and He is just, He will always honor His word by caring for and protecting His citizens because He desires for His kingdom to grow and bring in more citizens.

PREPARATION GENERATES MOMENTUM

"And from the days of John the Baptist until now, the kingdom of heaven suffereth violence, and the violent take it by force."
[Matthew 11:12]

Ellicott's Commentary for English Readers describes the violence spoken of in this scripture as "the eager rush of the crowds of Galilee and Judaea. It was, as it were, a city attacked on all sides by those who were eager to take possession of it." This is the type of violent force that you must possess and demonstrate as you seek after your promise. It is the men and women who possess a burning desire to satisfy their hunger and thirst for this promise that will be have a testimony to share about their exploits. However, the force needed to violently seize the promise can never be realized if you fail to produce momentum in your life.

Momentum is a physics term, but often used when in sports.

Although I had my struggles in science, I do recall the different mathematical formulas used in physics. The term momentum refers to the quantity of motion possessed by a certain object. Sir Isaac Newton defined momentum as "mass in motion." All objects have mass. So, if an object is moving, it has momentum, and now we have mass in motion. For example, a team exhibiting momentum is on the move and difficult to stop. I'm sure you have seen some teams that seem practically unbeatable. Due to the momentum generated, the team becomes an unyielding force that barrels over every obstacle in its path.

Typically in sports, when someone describes a team as having momentum, they are often referring to their offensive prowess. Why are they referring to the offense and not the defense? It is simply impossible for you to generate any kind of sustained momentum when your movement is solely dictated by your opponent's actions. It is the offensive minded who make their opponents worry about them, rather than them worrying about their opponent. They are constantly on the attack, deliberately executing their game plan in hopes to draw closer to their ultimate goal. The tam's success in executing the game plan was directly related to their preparation for the game.

Notice I said they prepared for the game, and not the opponent. The team prepares for the game, not their opponents. Opponents will always exist; they are there to resist you from attaining your promise. Yet, your focus cannot be on your opponent, but should be on the game. You must realize, your opponents or obstacles will change, but the game remains the same. Since the game remains the same, every team must establish an identity or a systematic approach to each game that imposes their will on their opponents. This is why sports teams spend months of preparation and training prior to the start of their season. The repetitive rehearsal of play after play instills a level of commitment to excellence in the pursuit of a prize. The period of preparation for the team is used to establish consistency and focus to the task at hand.

Focus: follow on the same course until successful. This mentality breeds an attitude of consistency. The ability to become consistent simply means you are able to establish an unchanging attitude or behavior over a period of time for a specific achievement. In your preparation, you must be consistent in your approach, attitude and actions. Consistency is a must! Regardless of your present condition and situation, your attitude must be aligned with the vision of the image of you possessing your promise, which you remain attentively focused on. The preparation you employ must be consistent and intentional. If you decide to follow the same course until you taste success, your preparation will be consistently intentional.

It is your consistency that produces your momentum. This momentum is developed in your steady pursuit with an unwavering attitude towards the capture of your promise, coupled with the deep assurance of it coming to pass. People with this kind of mentality are consistent in their approach and attack, likened unto a leaky faucet. Although the leaky faucet generates an irritating sound as the drip builds and persists, the water bill begins to grow out of control. The affect of something as small as a drop of water builds to a waterfall over time. Your consistency must be evident in your preparation, showing up in the exercising of your faith and your unwavering attitude. This will yield the much needed impetus to begin moving you closer to your promise.

Ultimately, the consistent behavior that bred this positive momentum has now produced a force to be reckoned with. This produced force is the much-needed energy to overcome every obstacle that stands in the way of you seizing your promise. This type of momentum is powerful and destructive, but the best thing is that it becomes your ally and best friend. The positive momentum positions the wind at your back and pushes you into the things of God that you envisioned in times past. For all the things that seemed to have been delayed, and when it seemed as if you were in walking in quick sand, you now begin to experience the fruitfulness of positive movement. It is a wonderful feeling to witness with your own two eyes the things you are able to accomplish with your two hands.

I recall when I purchased my first home. Every little phase of the building process made home ownership more of a reality on a daily basis, while becoming familiar with the weight of responsibility being levied on me. I was so giddy that it became a part of my everyday conversation. My house this, my house that. You could not stop me from talking about the house. I'm sure my friends and family were tired of my single-threaded conversations. In so much, I began shopping for things for the house at least six months before it was said to be ready. I bought new dishes, furniture, linen and silverware, storing away unnecessary things for my current living situation, to enable me to securely enjoy my future home. At times I felt foolish, thinking that I was going overboard and not making wise decisions. One day, I surveyed my current living condition and saw all of the dishes and linen which seemed to have overtaken me, maybe because it looked as if it had no use. As I stepped back and realized, every purchase I made was actually very needed for the home. Many of my possessions were no longer serviceable, and who wants to take old things into a new house?

Now, I am certainly not advocating for you to go out and spend unnecessary funds, or to make foolish decisions. However, I believe you should be wise concerning your future promise. I knew I was going to a new home, a place that no one else had ever laid their head. This was a home designed especially for me. So, I began to work a principle I found in scripture as a child that I now understood. *"Neither is new wine put into old wineskins [bottles]. If it is, the skins [bottles] burst and the wine is spilled and the skins [bottles] are destroyed. But new wine is put into fresh wineskins [bottles], and so both are preserved."* [Matt 9:17] Understanding this principle, and trusting it, I did not want any of the newness of the home to be marred by introducing old things and old ways to it. Please do not misunderstand me, it was not about the new dishes and furniture; all those things are perishable and can be replaced. Yet, it was about the new attitude and perspective I had adorned, which caused me to see life and the promise of a new home totally differently.

This mindset enabled me to work a principle in my life so that the principle would now work through my life. I trusted this truth insomuch that it shifted how I discussed the construction process with the builder. I became more involved in the building process, sharing specific ideas and concerns about what was taking place before my eyes. I visited the work site at least 3-4 times during the week, and I always showed up on the weekend to speak with the skilled professionals to obtain understanding of their methods and techniques. I was so involved that I had them making multiple changes until they reproduced the vision I imagined in my mind. I did this so often, the workers began to expect my arrival and approval for each of the completed phases.

Notice, I said my mindset had to change. I soon developed an attitude that coincided with my future state, rather than continuing to dwell in the past or present. This is necessary to maintain your momentum. Momentum is difficult to sustain when you keep shifting and turning. Think about it: when you're driving your car, to make a turn without risking life or limb, you typically reduce speed by removing your foot from the accelerator before applying pressure to the brake. Likewise, when driving a manual vehicle, to shift from one gear to the next, you must take your foot off of the gas and press the clutch prior to increasing speed. Both are necessary, but should be done with consideration and skill to optimize performance.

By holding true to this principle, it actually sped up my moving process. It allowed me to rid myself of many old and outdated things that no longer had value in my life, and they certainly had no value to coexist with my delivered promise. Everything in this phase of my life shall speak to my future, not my past. To add, I was able to move into a new home with minimum moving and decoration expenses once it was all said and done. As I became involved in the process from the start, the momentum I generated reduced every mountain presented to a leveled plain, thus expediting the delivery of my promise.

I never allowed naysayers to interfere with my momentum. Oftentimes we allow others to talk us out of our promises because people see things in the natural yet God does things in the supernatural. Do not allow family members, friends, co workers, church congregants, neighbors, acquaintances, enemies, humans, dogs, cats or rats to deter you from being diligent about your pursuit of your purpose! I never let a contractor, an architect, a bricklayer or a naysayer stop me from me having input on the promise of my home. In the end, they not only knew I would be coming but respected me for it!

If you have been given a promise, please get involved with God early in the process. Prayer should become a main ingredient of your daily diet. You should spend time in prayer reminding God about the promise, and asking God for clarity concerning it. The more you commune with God, the more you will come to understand God's purpose and plans for your life. God is a specific God, and trust is a prerequisite for your prayers to be answered. If you fail to trust God, your desire and excitement to run will soon diminish. Since God usually does not give us the entire picture in one setting, it is highly unlikely God would be very generic in the promise and instructions required to birth it. For this reason, it makes it ever more vital for you to remain in lock step with God through your journey that your momentum can continue to soar.

———— ○ ● ○ ————

It is pertinent for you not to allow your emotions to overwhelm you, but remaining obedient to the Holy Spirit for the blessings of the Lord to overtake you.

———— ○ ● ○ ————

You must understand, by spending time in prayer and preparing my life for the new home, I was not running towards the promise. Although the promise was ahead of me and not behind, and all of the dishes, furniture and linen were purposed for the house, I was learning obedience. I was learning discipline. I was learning submissiveness. My preparation was neither random nor logical. I asked God for a home that would not become a financial burden nor introduce stress into my life. So, I did not go out to purchase one thing before seeking the Lord. It may sound mundane or frivolous in nature but the process prepared me to deal with the road ahead. No, I was not running towards the promise of a new home, instead I was running towards the One who promised me the new home.

The preparation that generated the momentum to purchase a newly constructed home took me right past the home to a deeper relationship with God. *"Trust in the Lord with all thy heart, and lean not to your own understanding"* [Proverbs 3:5]. The momentum developed during this phase of my life was to trust the Lord despite the obstacles, naysayers, setbacks, and any other deterrents that may present itself while waiting for your promise. It was a blind trust, because I literally did not believe I could accomplish this on my own. Yet, I was right. God had his hand in every aspect of the process, thus making it much easier to handle. If you are going to lay claim to your long awaited promise, you must begin producing momentum that draws you closer to God through your unwavering faith and trust to prepare for that which He said He would not only do, but also deliver into your life.

PREPARATION PRODUCES PATIENCE

"And when they were come in, they went up into an upper room, where abode both Peter, and James, and John, and Andrew, Philip, and Thomas, Bartholomew, and Matthew, James the son of Alphaeus, and Simon Zelotes, and Judas the brother of James." [Acts 1:13]

If your father gave you a promise, would you believe him? How would you respond? Would you believe him? Would the hearing of the promise produce excitement in your life? If so, how long before the excitement expires? How often would you remind yourself or your father of the promise?

All of these questions are worthy of an answer. Although we may have never considered each question, they are all things each of us have done either as children or as adults. I can remember being a young teenager in my freshman year of high school when my father made a promise to me. I was a young high school football player who did not attend summer workouts. During summer workouts, the first players in attendance receive priority selection of the equipment and shoes.

Have you ever been given a promise that you desired so bad you could taste it? When you first receive word of your promise, you immediately begin to imagine it. You begin to see yourself in your promise. You believe in this so much that you dream about it; you actually find yourself lying waiting for it day after day. At first, it's exciting; it gives you a sense of purpose and exuberance as you have something to look forward to on a daily basis. You can replay those words over and over in your mind as if it just occurred. Unfortunately, the promise does not appear in your desired timeline. Days turn to weeks, weeks to months, and months to years. After a period of time, the idea of your promise begins to fade. The words, which once rang loudly in your ears, have now been muffled by life, situations and present circumstances. Now, anxiety starts to penetrate your mind, and everything that once reminded you of the promise now causes you to question yourself and the one who issued the promise.

On one hand, you may exclaim that you have waited patiently for your promise. On the other, you must answer the question if you have done anything to bring this promise closer to becoming a reality. You have dreamed but have you worked? You have prayed and cried have you made room for it? Simply put, have you prepared for your promise?

Simply put, preparation is not only an act of faith, but it is your faith in action. You should post a sign in your room stating, "Caution: Faith in Action!" Your faith in action is the evidence of the hope burning within you that drives you towards your destiny. Your faith, or strong belief in the deliverance of this promise, should prompt you to begin to prepare for its arrival. The preparation is the function of making ready your life for the very thing that you truly believe will show up in your life. Regardless of whether you have doubt concerning when and how it will appear, you must take the initiative to begin restructuring your life to for the promise that is on its way.

For example, if you were planning to hold a dinner party at your house, when would you decide to prepare for your guests? Would your preparation be dependent upon your like or dislike for your guests? Maybe it is dependent upon how much trust you have in the word of your guests. We all have friends and family who have let us down time after time. Do you prepare as if they have already arrived or do you wait for your guests to provide you another confirmation of their attendance? If you have found your guests to be trustworthy individuals who have always kept their word, why would you need another confirmation of their attendance? The relationship should be such that they would inform you if they were unable to attend, or even if plans have changed. You should move forward as if all systems are a go for the party.

Patience is a virtue! Not only it is a virtue, it is a characteristic of the fruit of the Holy Spirit made available to every believer in Christ to develop and partake of once Jesus ascended to sit at the right hand of the Heavenly Father. The kind of patience we should desire and seek after is the patience Job exhibited during his tribulations. Job demonstrated an enormous amount of resolve after suffering the loss of his children and livestock. To add insult to injury, he suffered great financial loss and could have fallen into a never-ending pit of depression, but his staying power became evident as he strengthened his communication and relationship with God.

It is unclear whether Job was cognizant to glory in his tribulation *"knowing that tribulations worketh patience; and patience, experience, and experience hope: and hope maketh not ashamed; because the love of God is shed abroad in our hearts by the Holy Ghost which is given unto us."* [James 1:3] His tribulations were psychologically and physically intensive, trying his patience every waking moment of his day. How could he remain patient in God if he did not believe in God? Job had to believe in God as his source, sustainer, and most of all, the God who restores. As his patience was tested, it allowed for his experience to exert his hope for a turnaround. This hope was not just for the pain and discomfort to vanish, but also for a new structure to be created in his life.

Patience is the capacity to accept or tolerate delay, regardless of the conditions and time period. It is the ability to wait, and remain comfortable and enthusiastic while you are waiting. This is a key contributor to the attitude you develop, and the maturation of your faith while on this journey to obtain your promise. Patience is so important because it exposes what lies within during times of difficulty or silence.

The pressure of the condition or situation becomes as a car compactor. Just as the car compactor crushes cars into cubes or pancakes, the pressure of the condition caused by the delay is applied in an attempt to crush your dreams of seizing your promise. The pressure applied to your life tends to be an excruciating pain and cause great discomfort. As the pressure slowly grinds into your life, it is quite unsettling which makes you become anxious and unstable. It can give the allusion of feeling trapped and unable to escape. Wait! Remember, this attempt is only an illusion the enemy wants to use to alter your focus. The enemy tries to use time and various detours as distractions to exert pressure. I charge you to stand up on the word of God spoken over your life. You shall live and not die, and the Lord will perfect that which concerns you. God is not going to allow any of the anointing and joy to be squeezed out of your life. This test is only a proving ground for the next dimension of your life, calling forth a greater depth of your faith in God. Your faith should enable you to remain focused on God and not the condition or situation. Your faith should be as a water skier attached to a boat by a line, navigating you through the waters. Regardless of the various obstacles and waves in the waters, as the skier, your responsibility is to hold tight to the line and keep your eyes focused on the boat guide.

Ultimately, one can never conquer the test of patience because each issue requires a greater level of patience. Yet, you can accept the test and be awarded to the Dean's List for exceptional performance if you conquer the level that you are on and the patience needed for that level.

PREPARATION HELPS POSITION YOU

CHANGE IS NECESSARY!

The practical application of preparation in your life literally moves you from one position to another. As you begin to prepare for something, it removes you from the starting line. It causes an energetic force to ignite within you to push you from a place of barrenness to a place of fruitfulness. The realization of fruitfulness occurs as you initiate the process, embarking upon a journey to surpass the crabs in the barrel. The moment you commence the first act of preparation towards your promise, you have caused your promise to shift closer to your present state. Maybe we can identify with the story of the woman with the issue of blood in the Bible.

"And a certain woman, which had an issue of blood twelve years, And had suffered many things of many physicians, and had spent all that she had, and was nothing bettered, but rather grew worse, When she had heard of Jesus, came in the press behind, and touched his garment. For she said, If I may touch but his clothes, I shall be whole. And straightway the fountain of her blood was dried up; and she felt in her body that she was healed of that plague. And Jesus, immediately knowing in himself that virtue had gone out of him, turned him about in the press, and said, Who touched my clothes? And his disciples said unto him, Thou seest the multitude

thronging thee, and sayest thou, Who touched me? And he looked round about to see her that had done this thing. But the woman fearing and trembling, knowing what was done in her, came and fell down before him, and told him all the truth. And he said unto her, Daughter, thy faith hath made thee whole; go in peace, and be whole of thy plague."[Mark 5:25-34]

Medically speaking, the woman was suffering with a prolonged menstruation for 12 years. According to the Law, she was rendered ritually unclean and had to remain in her home during her menstrual period. Under normal conditions, a woman would only be confined to her home for five to seven days, offering to her a time of rest and recovery to all that she does throughout the month. However, this was much different than a usual menstrual cycle. This woman had endured this issue constantly for more than 4,380 days. This natural cleansing process for the female body had now become an issue for this woman. What once was a regular, natural cleansing process that she was able to previously manage has now elevated and morphed to become a burden in her life and her social status.

A typical five to seven day period of rest and enjoying her home had become an imprisonment for her. The Law pertaining to purity which once worked in her favor, has now turned the tide and was working against her. During the time of a Jewish woman's menstrual period, she was relieved of many of her typical responsibilities. She no longer had to draw and carry water from the well. Her cooking duties for the family were not required, nor did she have to go to the marketplace. She could not have sexual intercourse, nor be among other people (Leviticus 15:19-31). She could not even touch the members of her family, or enjoy a normal life. These laws worked very well for healthy women with a normal menstrual period. Yet, they were backfiring for her and working against her life in her pursuit of a happy life. There were times in her life when she probably looked forward to having her quiet time or taking a break from her responsibilities. Now however, she was relegated to a permanent quiet life, confined to her home. In short, she was now a social leper!

As a result of her condition, the woman's position and status changed. She spent all her money to meet with every physician who would listen to her. One could imagine how she sought after the best physicians in the region, year after year, trying to rectify the matter. Yet, time after time, remedy after remedy, she suffered another defeat. Have you ever been there? Maybe it was not a doctor you sought, but a preacher or prophet, a counselor, a loan, a job, a child, but again and again, you came up empty. You mustered up enough strength to turn the knob of the door and walk through it with so much expectation, to leave feeling dejected as if the wind was stolen from your sails.

—————— ○ ● ○ ——————

...if you stay ready, you will never have to get ready.

—————— ○ ● ○ ——————

In those days, 1st century Palestine doctors used a wide range of herbal cures for their patients. Today, we have access to all kinds of medical aides and technologies. Regardless of the technological advances, there are some things that still only come about through "fasting and praying." Her funds were depleted, and her tolerance for shenanigans was at an all time low. Yet, she had at least a grain of faith to believe that a miracle-worker possessed the promise of her healing within Him.

Have you ever encountered a situation where the things that used to work for you in times past became a hindrance? The laws and rules that were made to protect you are now persecuting you. Please allow me to remind you, this is not the end of her story, just like it is not the end of yours. There is still something greater on the other side of this issue. Instead of giving up, begin to press through the crowd of adversity. The woman had reached the end of her rope and made a decision that deified the very thing that went from protecting her to imprisoning her.

She decided to change her position! She remembered that only those who subject themselves to the Law of Moses are the children of God. This means that along with every Law that instructed her to assume a position of aloneness and quietness during her menstrual period, was a promise of healing and redemption. The woman no longer looked unto man to rid her of the chains bondage, but rather the Lord of the promise to heal her infirmity. Notice how man's blood imprisoned her, while the Blood of Lamb liberated her! Her realization of who she was as a child of God, spiritually positioned her to receive her miracle. The crawling and pressing through the crowd was the physical aspects of the exercising of her faith that brought a wholeness in her life. If she had not changed her position, she would not have touched her promise. This change of position granted her the divine opportunity to touch and lay hold of her PROMISE!

This woman prepared herself to get as low as possible to receive the promise of healing. She prepared herself mentally prior to executing her plan. I do not believe it was a random act of desperation, but a calculated act of hopefulness. Long before she stepped a foot outside of her dwelling place that had now become her prison, and even before she saw the crowd, she envisioned herself crawling in the dirt amongst the people. The things she heard of Jesus, and all the mighty signs and wonders delivered by his hands, caused her to realize that after 12 years if Jesus could not deliver a promise of healing, it would never be. With the people having knowledge of her present condition, she knew the obstacles before her if she would merely attempt to take a stroll to meet Jesus face to face. Therefore she prepared herself to get as low as possible to the ground, and crawl as far as she could until she met the power of God wrapped in flesh. Amidst the crowd and dirt, people stepping on and over her, she was determined to get to the Promise! Nothing stopped her, nor was she bothered by the numerous feet that may have crushed the bones in her hands, legs or feet. She remained determined and positioned to encounter her Promise!

Although Jesus was heading in another direction and focused on someone else's issue, she was determined to catch Him. Instead of waiting for the Promise to find and overtake her, she sought out with determination to overtake her Promise! In this season, you must make a conscious decision and effort to position yourself to overtake your promise. In this text, Jesus was the woman's Promise! What position must you take to get to your promise? Will you need to humble yourself and submit to a mentor? Maybe you need to work for someone else for a period of time prior to God releasing you to launch your own business. Do you need to become a giver so your windows of opportunity can be opened in order for you to receive? Take the time to seek the Lord on what change needs to be made to prepare to receive your promise.

RECEIVE YOUR HELP

"The promise of a helper fit for you! So the Lord God caused

a deep sleep to fall upon the man, and while he slept took one of his ribs and closed up its place with flesh. And the rib that the Lord God had taken from the man he made into a woman and brought her to the man." [Gen 2:21-23]

After God created Adam and placed him in the Garden of Eden, God made a critical observation. God, Himself said, "It is not good that the man should be alone." In other words, the work I have assigned to Adam's hand to perform and be responsible for is too great for one man to accomplish alone. The vision God has given you is too great for one set of human hands to work alone. There are great and awesome things God has deposited in each and every one of us. Yet, it will not achieve its full manifestation until the divine assistance God has ordained comes along side of us. It is not the will of God for us to be in the field alone, straining, striving and stressing over a work that extends far greater than your eyes can see.

Maybe it's fine for you to be alone if you promised yourself something but if God placed something inside of you, then you're going to need help. For example, consider you launched out to start your own business. On day one, you have just assumed the role and responsibilities of chief executive officer, chief financial officer, executive assistant, quality assurance officer (janitor), parking attendant, director of marketing, director of public relations, and anything else required for the business to operate. To add further complexities to the thought, you are married with a child. If this seems like an abundance of duties and responsibilities, it is! It is tiresome just thinking about all the things that may be required. When do you have time to build and grow your business? You become so overwhelmed with performing in your functional day-to-day duties, it becomes practically impossible for you to design any sound business strategies and practices.

So, here we have a man created by the very hands of God, with the very oxygen of God in his nostrils, and God said it was not good for him to be alone in the work he was created to do. This was Adam in the Garden of Eden. He was everything to the garden. Adam worked every aspect of the land he was given. Day and night, night and day, he tended to every fabric of his territory by himself. Sadly enough, there are many of us who are still trying to work and carry every square inch of the thing God has given us. Fortunately, God stopped and observed His creative works and determined "It is not good that the man should be alone." Therefore, God's work was not done with Adam. There was yet a promise suspended in the atmosphere waiting to be manifested. This too is your story. There is yet a promise suspended in the atmosphere waiting to be manifested in order to help complete a work!

God knew man needed a suitable mate to partner with him for the work He assigned him to do. God however allowed Adam to meet every living creature first. I believe God wanted to see whether Adam knew and understood who he was created to be. Adam could then recognize who God's creations were intended to be in his life prior to releasing his promise. Adam was able to maintain his position as a son of God, so he could receive his woman of God. The very thing Adam needed was already in him. Adam just had to stop, rest in God, and allow God to pull her out of him.

Can we say reproduce! Proper positioning enables and empowers us the ability to reproduce! It affords us the benefits and opportunities to see all there is to offer from a greater vantage point, not having to work for things, but allowing things to work for and through us. As children, our parents teach us how to do while helping us along the way. Their responsibility is to nurture us, help us discover and shape our identity, and prepare us for life ahead. Parents possess more life experiences and a collaboration with their children enables us to accomplish and achieve things in a greater capacity as we operate in harmony. If done properly, it is multiple generations working in concert to produce a promise in the earth at an appointed time.

For God to get the promise out of Adam, Adam had to enter a position of rest. I cannot imagine Adam experiencing difficulties with allowing God to place him into a deep sleep, especially since Adam knew God as his Creator. Adam completely trusted his Creator, so he was able to rest his life in his hands. The rest we must enter into with God is a sign of confidence and faith in the One who holds us. When we lie on our beds, are we timid that the bed cannot support our weight? If so, it is time for a new bed! Rather, we rest comfortably feeling assured when we rise we will be ready for the day and challenges ahead. I encourage you to do as Adam. Rest in the Lord and allow Him to pull your promise out of you!

———————— ○ ● ○ ————————

It requires insight and foresight to discount your present day realities and start preparing for your next day actualities.

———————— ○ ● ○ ————————

After Adam completed his assessment and named every living creature God had created, he realized that nothing fit his need. Adam was not able to find a complementary partner to fulfill his mission and purpose in the earth. There is something to be said for the person who has waited year after year, and date after date to find a spouse, and still unable to find someone who is like minded and desires the same things out of life. It is good to know that the assignment and vision birthed in you has not reached its full maturity. The very promise we have been waiting for lies within us; we merely have to allow God to place us in a position of rest.

Oftentimes, it is difficult for people to identify with Biblical figures or even listen to someone else's testimony or account. We regularly read the Bible, trying to understand the stories of Adam, Abraham, Isaac, Jacob, David and many others. We try to figure out whether it was truly God that moved in your friend's life. However, the reality is that "God is no respecter of persons" [Acts 10:34]. Do not spend your time focusing on whom God did it for, and what God did for them. Know that He can do it for you too! God just decided to start with someone to give the rest of us an example or role model for a point of reference. God had to provide us with several models to pattern our lives after which will lend hope and trust in the One who created us. When we come to acknowledge and understand this truth, it should help us rest in the truth that He will bring us to an expected end. God will deliver every promise which He issued concerning His chosen generation. It is the arrival of your absolute assurance that God is God, and no one can dispute His Will and Word for your life, and your children's lives.

POSITION IS SECURED IN CHRIST

"The Spirit itself beareth witness with our spirit, that we are the children of God: And if children, then heirs; heirs of God, and joint- heirs with Christ; if so be that we suffer with him, that we may be also glorified together."[Romans 8:16-17]

We as human beings place a great premium on social status. Our position in the family, on the job, in the community, in the church, or any other organizational infrastructure with a hierarchical design has been deemed worthy of our attention and fortitude. Daily, men and women claw, kill, steal, lie, cheat and any other unmentionable act necessary to get a leg up on their fellow man (or woman).

No matter the cost, at one time or another, each of us has done something dishonest to get a little closer to the person, place or thing we have desired in life. Think back; have you ever cut in line so you did not have to wait as long? What about befriending someone under false pretenses to gain unfair privileges that you otherwise would not receive? Have you arrived early for a class, church or even a seminar just to get the seat you wanted? These are forms of attempting to position oneself for an extraordinary advantage.

Irrespective of our current position in our families, households, jobs, ministry, or social organizations, as a believer in God, your position has been solidified. The positioning of one self as a child of God establishes you as an heir of God and a joint-heir with Christ. To be an heir merely means you have an inheritance coming to you. Simply put; as an offspring of your natural parents, you are lawfully engrafted into heir-ship. You do not have to do anything to deserve it. You earned it by simply being their child. In the spirit realm, you have earned you're your heir-ship by means of having the Father of all. What a wonderful place to be when you recognize that you are a child of God!

Sadly enough, many of us have yet to assume our predetermined positions in the kingdom of God, thus leaving us outside of the gates. When you are not aware or understand your position in Christ, it can render you powerless. It is as if you have been given a car without the keys. The only way you can start the car is through illegal tactics. We instantly become robbers and thieves due to our illegal practices not understanding how the kingdom of God operates. Until we realize that unless we assume a position of citizenship in God's kingdom, we will remain trapped in the religious bondage of traditions and dizzy rituals. I use the term dizzy because many of us have been running around in circles for years doing silly things that have no basis, nor have amounted to anything of substance that can attribute to God's handy work.

Since I am a child of the Most High God and a loyal citizen of His kingdom, I can begin to move legally towards my promise. Philippians 3:20 says, *"But our citizenship is in heaven, and from it we await a Savior, the Lord Jesus Christ."* Citizenship gives you rights and privileges to operate legally in a country. When you take your rightful place as a citizen in the kingdom of God, God authorizes you to legally move and operate in the earth. In fact, you literally become an agent for God in the earth, living out Jesus' declaration in Matthew 16:19: *"I will give you the keys of the kingdom of heaven, and whatever you bind on earth shall be bound in heaven, and whatever you loose on earth shall be loosed in heaven"* [ESV]. Take your rightful place and enjoy the citizenship you are authorized to enjoy! Move into position! Your promise awaits!

─────── ○ ● ○ ───────

I was not running towards the promise of a new home, instead I was running towards the One who promised me the new home.

─────── ○ ● ○ ───────

PROVOKE THE HEAVENS
TO RESPOND

PERSISTENCE AND RELENTLESSNESS

After you have prepared and remained patient, while exercising willingness and obedience, you now must be willing and able to provoke the Heavens. To provoke the Heavens means you are willing and able to position yourself to cause the hand of God to move over your life.

"And he spake a parable unto them to this end, that men ought always to pray, and not to faint; Saying, There was in a city a judge, which feared not God, neither regarded man: And there was a widow in that city; and she came unto him, saying, Avenge me of mine adversary. And he would not for a while: but afterward he said within himself, Though I fear not God, nor regard man; Yet because this widow troubleth me, I will avenge her, lest by her continual coming she weary me. And the Lord said, Hear what the unjust judge saith. And shall not God avenge his own elect, which cry day and night unto him, though he bear long with them? I tell you that he will avenge them speedily. Nevertheless when the Son of man cometh, shall he find faith on the earth?" [Luke 18:1-8]

The parable of the persistent widow offers great insight to the type of attitude God expects of His people. This rendition of Jesus' lesson to the disciples is centered on consistency, persistence and relentless pursuit of what God said is rightfully yours. To provoke the judge to move on her behalf, the widow understood the need to be consistent and relentless in her pestering. This required an attitude of persistence and an absolute reluctance to accept things as they have been presented to her. She realized that what she was seeing in her present day was not the vision of how she saw her life. She made up her mind that she would not stop pestering and pleading with the judge until she got what she needed! She sought for vengeance from her adversaries, and she did not allow the judge to rest until he met her request. How relentless are you in your pursuit?

First, Jesus identifies this woman as a widow. He does not provide a name, the city or region she resided, if she has any children, nor did He provide her issue. The only thing Jesus disclosed concerning the woman was that she was a widow, had an adversary, and that she requested for her judge to avenge her. Come to think of it, Jesus does not even share with the disciples how long she has been plagued by this adversary. In teaching this lesson, Jesus only shared the facts. This is an example of Jesus helping the disciples to remain focused on the facts. Do not get caught up in the details! Have you ever heard the phrase? "The devil is in the details." Similar to disciples, we must remain focused on the facts concerning the lesson. The woman's husband was dead and she no longer had anyone to fight on her behalf. With her being a widow, all she had was what she had. The laws and customs did not permit her to provide for herself. Did I remember to mention that the woman was a widow? Meaning, she was economically, socially and legislatively powerless! According to their laws and customs, this woman had no voice. Her inheritance, resources, social influence and any kind of future were buried along with her husband.

Why would Jesus not include the woman's name in the story? Maybe the woman already had a charge against her for a prior misdemeanor or felony. Could she have been named in a criminal investigation? Could her family name have disqualified her as a result of their fortunes or misfortunes? Maybe the sins of the father and mother seemingly keep us from going before the judge. Maybe the shear meaning of her name could have given the allusion that she would be unqualified to see the judge. Jesus did not disclose the woman's name because He wanted the disciples to know and understand that anyone can go to the Judge. Whether you have an issue large or small, day or night, lasting for a days, weeks, months or years, the Heavenly Judge is willing and able to satisfy your claim.

The lack of recognition of the city the woman lived in reminds us that our location cannot disqualify us from being heard by the Judge. Jesus wanted the disciples to know that regardless of which side of the tracks they derived or currently resided, they have every right and privilege to the same access to the Judge. So do you and I! Oftentimes, we allow the shame and embarrassment of where we're from to keep us from taking our concerns and issues to the Judge, Great Jehovah.

Probably, the most important thing about the persistent widow going to the judge every day was not mentioned in the parable yet it was implied. How can someone repeatedly go before a judge? How does one gain this type of access? The widow must have known and understood the Law and how to approach the judge. She must have possessed a knowledge and understanding of the Law for the judge to hear her petition. The widow must have known and understood the Laws of the land, how they protected her, and how the Law benefited her life.

You may also have found yourself in the same type of condition. Your husband or wife may not have died, but you have allowed your promise of a better life to expire. The very thought of that thing that was so precious gave you passion and strength to rise in the morning with vigor and a sense of expectation. The very idea or image of this promise caused your eyes to light up. The idea caused you to press your way towards the door of life. You were hoping the light of a new day would expose the very thing that has remained hidden from you for all this time. Day after day, month after month, year after year, you witness a let down. You enter the day with such an abundance of excitement about the possibilities that lie ahead, but by day's end, your head is directed southward with gloom and despair.

Maybe you are not a widow but your economic and social status is marred, and the judicial or legislative systems will not hear your case. The lawyers have even told you that you do not have any grounds or merit to win. Neither banks, friends nor family will give you a loan. It seems as if every time you move forward, a door or window of opportunity is slammed in your face. I want to encourage you that God is still on the throne, and He is the Judge over your life. You will receive that which God has promised you! If you are willing to remain persistent, and develop a relentless attitude about your promise and chase after the Judge day after day, your answer; your justice; your harvest will be granted unto you!

One of the things I love about this story is how the judge describes the widow's persistence. In the American Standard Version, the judge makes this statement in the fifth verse, *"yet because this widow troubleth me, I will avenge her, lest she wear me out by her continual coming."* Notice the judge is concerned about the widow wearing him out with her continual persistence. This widow was relentless! Although the judge was concerned about him becoming worn out by the widow, the judge's responses did not birth any doubt, frustration or weariness on the widow's part. Rather, she possessed an unyielding durability to repeatedly plead her case to the judge. I do not know exactly what the widow woman said to the judge, but she said and did it religiously and relentlessly. She made sure the judge heard her voice and her issue on a regular basis. I bet she did it so often that the judge could almost state the time the widow woman would arrive with the same case and attitude.

You cannot get tired! Your willingness and desire to plead your case to the Judge must become deliberate and uncompromising! Regardless of the hour, day, week, month or year, your goal should be to remind God of your promise as often as possible. Your strategy in approaching your Judge is to plead your case through the word of God. Remind God of His promise to you. You must fortify your mind, attitude and speech to drive unrelenting actions to present you before the One with all power and authority to change and transform your life situations. When you remind God of His word and His promises, you incite Him to respond because God has placed His word above His name. In other words, God will always honor His word!

Can you imagine the widow woman standing before the judge and saying, "In the case of Smith vs Smith, you acquitted them of all the charges! I too am a loyal citizen of the kingdom! If you did it for them, then you can do it me!" When was the last time you invoked your citizenship rights granted to you by the blood of Jesus Christ for God's kingdom? You need to remind yourself that as a child of God, a citizen of the kingdom of God, it is not legal for you to be poor. It is not legal for you to face defeat! It is not legal for you to be lacking for anything! If you are a citizen of the kingdom of God, God is your Judge and you must utilize His Law to get that which He has promised you.

PUSH UNTIL YOU BREAKTHROUGH

Are you aware that in every promissory note or agreement, there is an acceleration clause? A promissory note is simply an agreement between a lender and a borrower outlining terms of a "promise to pay." The acceleration clause is included, sometimes in smaller print, typically found on the back of the agreement. This acceleration clause outlines special parameters or circumstances that allows the lender to require immediate payment of all money due if certain conditions occur before the time that payment would otherwise be due.

This is great news! It is a guarantee to both you and I that my payment of my promise can be accelerated. Since God never starts a work that He hasn't already finished, I then become responsible for influencing the conditions to change that will evoke an immediate payment. This is what Elijah did in 1 Kings 18. God already said it would not rain for three years. Now he finds himself in the third year and sees not an inkling of precipitation in the atmosphere. Elijah understood God so much that he knew there was an acceleration clause in the agreement, so he pushed and pushed until the promise of a rain breakthrough into the atmosphere.

"And Elijah said unto Ahab, Get thee up, eat and drink; for there is the sound of abundance of rain. So Ahab went up to eat and to drink. And Elijah went up to the top of Carmel; and he bowed himself down upon the earth, and put his face between his knees. And he said to his servant, Go up now, look toward the sea. And he went up, and looked, and said, There is nothing. And he said, Go again seven times. And it came to

pass at the seventh time, that he said, Behold, there ariseth a cloud out of the sea, as small as a man's hand. And he said, Go up, say unto Ahab, Make ready thy chariot, and get thee down, that the rain stop thee not."[1 Kings 18:41-44]

Provoking the heavens to respond is a must when you've found yourself in a holding pattern for an extended period of time. You may find yourself asking the question, "God when is this going to happen?" Before you tune out because you believe this is blasphemous, take a moment to consider Elijah's predicament during the drought and the persistent widow previously discussed. I don't believe it is a coincidence that both accounts are found in the eighteenth chapter in the books of 1 Kings and Luke respectively. In the Bible, the number eighteen in the Hebrew language often symbolized the end of testing, a new beginning, and life. The Hebrew letters that make us the number 18 are Cheth, which is also the Hebrew number 8 and Yod, which is the Hebrew number 10. When combined, the two numbers make the number 18, and these Hebraic letters spell the word for life, which Chay. According to the Strong's Hebrew dictionary, Chay (pronounced khah-ee) literally means alive, raw, fresh, strong, life.

For example, in Luke 13:16, we find a woman being bound with an infirmity or illness for eighteen years. After one encounter with Jesus, she was given a new beginning, a new life through the delivering power of Jesus Christ. Also on two separate occasions, the Israelites were oppressed by their enemies for a period of eighteen years (Judges 3:14; 10:8). The people remained in oppression until God rose up a deliverer to bring an end to it and give them a fresh new beginning.

Now, both the Prophet Elijah and the persistent widow understood faith was the key ingredient to resolve their issue. Simply put, they trusted and believed the One they were petitioning had the power and authority to change their conditions. As difficult as it may have seemed, while all around them may have considered them to be somewhat delusional, they remained consistent in their faith in God's ability to deliver on His promise.

Now Elijah and Israel were in the midst of an elongated drought. This was not a mere three or six month drought most of us experience during summers living in America. This drought perpetuated. The drought lasted three years. As a result of the drought, the region was experiencing a famine. The people and the land were experiencing death, starvation, scarcity of goods and the wells began to dry up.

Most notably, from 2010 to 2012, Somalia endured a horrendous famine. The famine was so devastating that it took the lives of nearly 260,000 men, women and children. The food shortage stole the lives of nearly 2.6% of Somalia's population, impacting generations of families within the country. The sad thing about the famine in Somalia was that they saw it coming and were late to respond. Studies show that close to half of deaths occurred prior to the famine being declared. This means that the people were already in the famine before their government acknowledged their need for assistance. God help us to identify leaders with insight and foresight so that we can plan and prepare for that which is ahead. As you see, a famine can wipe out an entire nation if you are not prepared. You must not allow your promise to starve from lack of preparation.

Here is Elijah, a man that predicted the drought, but now understands that it is time for the drought to come to an end. He senses in his spirit that the season of depravity and dryness is now exiting stage left. Elijah declared to King Ahab and into the atmosphere that *"There is a sound of abundance of rain."* Now, you must know, there was no lightning or thundering occurring at the time he made this profound statement. I do not even believe Elijah could smell the rain in the air but he began to hear it in his spirit. He heard the sound of raindrops hitting the ground.

What do you hear in your spirit? Can you hear the sound of babies crying? Do you hear the crowds of people applauding as you stand before them delivering your performance? Can you hear the announcer calling your name to present your Grammy or Oscar Award? What can you hear in your spirit? When you begin to hear the sound of your promise in your spirit, it means it is time for you to get in the birthing position and began to push!

─────── ○ ● ○ ───────

Adam was able to maintain his position as a son of God, so he could receive his woman of God.

─── ○ ● ○ ───

This is where Elijah now finds himself. He is at a point where the sound in his spirit is urging and pulling him to position himself to make this sound a reality for all to hear and witness. Just as you are at this very moment preparing yourself for position and ready to push forth life! Elijah positioned himself as a woman with labor pains, feeling each contraction, one after another. Like a woman's cervix, his spirit is dilated. His spirit was so open that he had to place his head between his knees to ensure nothing in his sphere of influence could distract him from bringing forth this promise of rain.

Probably the most amazing part of this historical event was the report Elijah received from his servant. After his servant had gone out searching for rain six times with no sign of clouds, no evidence of moisture in the atmosphere, no cause for excitement, the seventh trip everything changed. Along this journey, we must ensure we are connected to people who will encourage, support and serve us even when there are no signs of rain, even when there is no sign of logic or sanity. Elijah was consistent with his request to the servant, and the servant was consistent in upholding his duty to Elijah. They worked as a team to deliver this baby!

Please allow me to pause for a second to shift the focus to the servant. Notice, the servant does not have a name. There is no mention of the servant's name and what the servant's role was to Elijah at this time. It is only written that he was being obedient; running, looking for rain. To birth this promise, you need people who aren't seeking after fame and fortune, or any kind of notoriety. The people who are connected to you must be selfless and desire to see your promise come to past just as much as you do. The greatest leader that ever walked the earth said, *"Even as the Son of Man came not to be served, but to serve"* [Matt 20:28 KJV].

Elijah may have been able to go down on his own, but it was important for him to remain in his position of birthing until the baby showed. You must remain in the position of prayer that provokes the living God to move on your behalf. He remained in this posture until the servant returned with the report he was waiting on. The servant saw *"a cloud the size of a man's hand coming out of the sea."* Elijah had pushed, and pushed, prayed, and prayed until his hand supernaturally broke through to the other side.

Elijah understood that God had already spoken concerning the rain. God's word is sovereign. Yet, God needed an agent in the earth to cooperate with heaven to produce the will of God in the earth, *"your will be done on earth as it is in heaven."* The pressure Elijah applied was the pressure of a supernatural force that was determined to give birth to something greater than him. He understood that the resistance he felt was life on the other side. The very thing you have been promised will birth into your life and bring forth a new life for you. This was true for Elijah and the nation of Israel. The famine was a result of the drought, and the drought affected everything that needed water for sustainment.

There is something in your life that requires the existence of your promise for sustainment. This "something" is in need of your promise to feed another area of your life. This "something" needs your promise so you can move forward into a new level, dimension and or realm of your life. Do not deterred by the resistance. The resistance is actually the evidence and assurance that there is life waiting for you on the other side of this journey, but it will not come easy. To lay hold of this promise, it is a necessity for you to apply Holy Ghost force to your prayers and actions. There must be a violent, Kingdom prayer life that ignites passion and desire so much in your life that those closest to you contract it and are impacted by it. *"The kingdom of heaven suffereth violence, and the violent take it by force"* [Matt 11:12 KJV].

LET'S POSSESS THE PROMISE

"Jehovah our God spake unto us in Horeb, saying, Ye have dwelt long enough in this mountain: turn you, and take your journey, and go to the hill- country of the Amorites, and unto all the places nigh thereunto, in the Arabah, in the hill-country, and in the lowland, and in the South, and by the sea-shore, the land of the Canaanites, and Lebanon, as far as the

great river, the river Euphrates. Behold, I have set the land before you: go in and possess the land which Jehovah swore unto your fathers, to Abraham, to Isaac, and to Jacob, to give unto them and to their seed after them." [Deuteronomy 1:6-8]

You've prepped your life, working to ensure you are in proper alignment with the will of God for your life. You have your business plan typed up and ready to go. You have resolved all your debt issues, and repaired your credit. You have purchased the basinet, and all the baby clothes the closet can handle. You have even purchased your tuxedo or wedding gown, along with the wedding bands, all in preparation for the big day. You have positioned yourself with God, prepared yourself mentally and practically, and executed fasting and prayer to the highest extent. Now that you have done all the things to prepare for the promise God has already declared is rightfully yours, it is now time to possess it! It is time to move and go after it!

This was Moses' attitude and mentality at the forty year juncture of their journey. Following forty years of tests and trials, living in the wilderness with no place to call home, it was finally time to posses the promise. Moses addresses the people with confidence and conviction about the path ahead. Moses' speech began with possessive language; Jehovah, our God! In order to take possession, to seize the thing that drives your desire, it first begins with a positive, assertive attitude. The attitude expected to be birthed out of this lecture is designed to produce optimism and kill the mentality and ideology of passivity, worry and negative thought patterns. It is time for the almost there people to be separated from the pack. Moses needed people who were ready and determined to finish what they began four decades ago. This type of attitude will begin to develop power in one's life to move you from aimless activities into purposeful movement. To attain this mindset, your daily experiences will be accompanied with constructive thought processes, extracting only the fruitful particles from every situation in life. These constructive thought processes will enable you to become more focused on the path ahead. No longer should you labor over minor set-backs and inopportune miscues. Instead, you should rejoice in the Lord in the smallest of victories thus strengthening you for the next conquest.

Moses was not merely repeating what he heard God say, but he was speaking what he knew God was about to do. It is great to recite and repeat God's word, or any other quotes that instigate positive thinking. However, if you lack belief and conviction in what you are saying, it is for not. If you lack belief or conviction, you may need to keep reciting it until your belief system is firmly rooted and planted in it. You will not be able to achieve the results you desire unless you are fully persuaded.

Moses was fully persuaded. He knew they had sojourned long enough in the wilderness. Moses' relationship was so tight and right with God that he knew without a shadow of a doubt that it was their time to possess the land. There comes a time in your walk that you should know unequivocally that God is about to move on your behalf. As the old folks use to say, you should know it in your *knower*. You have to know when your season of testing and trials has culminated, and when your season of celebration has commenced. As a matter of fact, you should start rejoicing now because God is giving you the plans and strategy to possess that which He has personalized and stored up just for you.

Once we are truly able to possess this positive attitude, it is now reflected in our speech. King Solomon tells us in Proverbs 18:21 that *"death and life are in the power of the tongue; and they that love it shall eat the fruit thereof."* Simply put, we have the power to produce and shape our world through the words that come from our mouth. Do not allow naysayers, Debbie-downers and doubt farmers to enter your sphere and convince you to stop speaking positive. The universe responds to the creative nature of our speech. Ludwig Wittgenstein, the Austrian-British philosopher said, *"The limits of my language mean the limits of my world."* In other words, the words we speak can be empowering and life changing, causing an atmospheric shift in our lives to either expand or collapse. Words can lift us to the greatest of heights, or tear us down to the point of making us feel completely useless and worthless. When I listen to the words of optimistic people, I feel as if their words are like the wings of eagles designed to carry me into another realm. My mind begins to take flight, and every word released from their mouth tells of a vision for my mind to rehearse and behold.

This further substantiates the necessity for the right attitude for one to move into possessing that which God has decreed is rightfully yours. If your attitude is the vine on which your words are connected and feeds, and your words are processed by your mind and clearly articulated by your mouth, then you will know they are truly derived from your heart. The word of God tells us in, *"for out of the abundance of the heart, the mouth speaks."* [Matthew 12:34]. As this truth begins to swell in your heart, it begins to birth positive, possessive words that will create and shape the psychological confidence to move forward into your new season. The releasing of these words from your mouth into the atmosphere can now reenter your ear gates and water the very seed this word yielded in your heart. The watering of these words will send neurological signals from your brain throughout your body, instructing it how and when to move. This is what we in the kingdom of God refer to as faith; *"faith comes by hearing, and hearing by the word of God."* [Rom 10:17] Faith moves us from merely dreaming about our promise, to talking about it, and eventually possessing it. It is the very evidence which our hope envisioned for months, and for many of us years. Faith is notifying you of God's constant presence in your life working on your behalf to deliver a promise designed specifically for you.

In this passage, Moses is speaking to a generation of people who were born in the wilderness. If you recall, these were a family of people who God chose to deliver from 400 years of slavery, removing them from under the thumb of the Egyptian Pharaoh. Now, these were not the very same Israelites who Moses led out of the enslavement of the Egyptians, but they were descendants of slaves. Like many people today, we are descendants of slaves, both naturally and spiritually. Fortunately, history has taught us that natural slavery typically has an expiration date. Or, the slave can build up the confidence to flee from his or her oppressor. Unfortunately, mental or spiritual slavery does not work the same way. This type of slavery takes years to break and de-program. This is why there are so many motivational speakers. Generations of people have been enslaved in their minds and spirits and have no clue they are in bondage. Today, I decree and declare that the chains of bondage are broken off your mind in the mighty name of Jesus! You will see God in a new light, causing you to see yourself in a new light!

This generation of Israelites grew up without homes, roaming around as nomads, but arguably having the best food ever known to man. Due to their unfaithfulness, the Israelites were sentenced to forty years of wandering in the wilderness. Do not be unfaithful to God! If you have slipped up, or not believed God at His word, apologize. Seek forgiveness and get back in right standing with God. You know the story. You have heard it time and time again, packaged in a variety of ways. A trip originally intended to take less than a week by foot, unleashed four decades of continuous cycles to bring a nation into total submission and servitude to the Almighty Creator. Moses was telling the people that the season of wandering is over! The expiration date has arrived for you to stop wandering. No longer will you move aimlessly without direction. The vagabond spirit [Gen 4:12] has been broken off of your life. No longer will you walk round and round in circles, because the Lord, your God, has declared it is over! For today, I am moving you forward into your destiny. Allow the Lord to be your Shepherd, the One who leads and guides, and directs you into the possession of your promise.

Through his series of speeches in Deuteronomy, Moses was preparing the children of Israel for possession, expansion, enlargement, and to receive the promise spoken over their lives before they were formed in their mothers' wombs. He was preparing their minds to make the necessary adjustments to live in their promised land. He instructed them to begin to walk around the land as if it was already theirs. This should help prompt you to begin to canvass about your promise, whether in your mind or in reality. I recall hearing a pastor say in one of his teachings that before he built his large church facility, he would visit one of the larger ministry's facilities in the local area and would envision himself preaching there in the pulpit. Then he went on to say that before he purchased a helicopter, he would visit the local dealer, and he began learning about the helicopter and became friends with one of the workers at the dealership. He was preparing his mind for what was to come. He had to know what it took to purchase the helicopter. What type of insurance was needed? How much he would need to pay a mechanic and pilot? What were the qualifications needed for a mechanic or pilot? Where would he keep the helicopter? He could not park it in his garage or on his front lawn. To take possession, or seize that promise, you have to begin to walk and live as if you already have it. You must prepare yourself mentally, so you can see yourself in your promise. Your mind must enlarge and expand to the capacity that it can hold some of the things God desires to make your life look like the kingdom of Heaven.

"Now Jericho was shut up inside and outside because of the people of Israel. None went out, and none came in. And the Lord said to Joshua, "See, I have given Jericho into your hand, with its king and mighty men of valor." [Joshua 6:1-2]

Now, for those of you who have already crossed over your Jordan River, you're almost there! You are standing at the brink of possessing your promise. You're within arm's length of your promise. For those who have circumcised themselves by the Sword, the Lord speaks to Joshua and says, *"See, I have given Jericho into your hand, with its king and mighty men of valor."* Although the city remains shut up, your obedience is going to open it to you. A walk of faith will bring down the impenetrable walls. A warring spirit will seize every kingdom that has set itself against you and our God to keep you out of your promise!

The sword is a weapon of war! For you and I, the sword represents the word of God. It is a multi-purposed sword. It is needed to circumcise our fleshly hearts, and war against our enemies. The Joshua generation is a warring generation. We cannot take possession unless you are prepared to war. You cannot war until you properly know and understand how to use your weapons.

"Finally, my brethren, be strong in the Lord, and in the power of his might. Put on the whole armour of God, that ye may be able to stand against the wiles of the devil. For we wrestle not against flesh and blood, but against principalities, against powers, against the rulers of the darkness of this world,

against spiritual wickedness in high places. Wherefore take unto you the whole armour of God, that ye may be able to withstand in the evil day, and having done all, to stand.

Stand therefore, having your loins girt about with truth, and having on the breastplate of righteousness; And your feet shod with the preparation of the gospel of peace; Above all, taking the shield of faith, wherewith ye shall be able to quench all the fiery darts of the wicked. And take the helmet of salvation, and the sword of the Spirit, which is the word of God: Praying always with all prayer and supplication in the Spirit, and watching thereunto with all perseverance and supplication for all saints." [Ephesians 6:10-18]

You are now out of the wilderness and at the brink of the city. You are at the brink of receiving your promise, the thing you have been waiting and praying and fasting and believing for!

Now that you are in position… Now that you are prepared… Now that you have demonstrated God-ward patience... It shall manifest!

Amen.

─────── ○ ● ○ ───────

The very promise we have been waiting for lies within us; we merely have to allow God to place us in a position of rest.

─────── ○ ● ○ ───────

THE END

ABOUT THE AUTHOR

Keith Garner, leader, visionary, entrepreneur, innovative thinker, military veteran and business strategist. Keith serves as an associate pastor at Renew Life Worship Center in Woodbridge, VA. He is a gifted leader, mentor and teacher, focused on the professional and spiritual development of the next generation of leaders.

Keith strives to be a leading voice of innovation, inspiration, and influence in the Body of Christ, as well as the world.

www.keithgarner.com